372.84| Coo

D0102261

MARINO INSTITUTE OF EDUCATION

Cracking Assemblies

72 Christian Assemblies
for Primary Schools

by Margaret Cooling and Diane Walker

Stapleford Centre Books

Acknowledgements

We would like to thank the following people for their help with different aspects of the project: Elaine Cooke, Robert Cooling, Ruth Cooper, Helen Johnson, Martyn Payne, Mike Skidmore, Helen Thacker, Robin Walker and Jon Webster. We would also like to express our gratitude to the various schools who allowed us to test this material.

Copyright. Margaret Cooling and Diane Walker 1998

The right of Margaret Cooling and Diane Walker to be identified as the authors of this work has been asserted by them in accordance with Copyright, Designs and Patents Act 1988.

First published 1998
Reprinted 1999
ISBN 0 9516537 8 4

British Library Cataloguing in Publication Data

A catalogue record for this book is available from the British Library.

The Stapleford Centre

Full details of courses and publications are available from The Stapleford Centre, Stapleford House, Wesley Place, Stapleford, Nottingham. NG9 8DP.

Note: we are grateful to Helen Thacker for the assembly on page 51

All rights reserved. No part of this book, with the exception of single copies of the illustrations, may be reproduced or transmitted in any form or by any means, electronic or mechanical, including photocopying, recording or by any information storage and retrieval system without permission in writing from the publisher or a licence permitting restricted copying in the United Kingdom issued by the Copyright Licensing Agency Ltd, 90, Tottenham Court Road, London W1P 9HE. Single photocopies of the illustrations may be made by the purchasing institution without further permission.

Cover design and internal illustrations by Jane Taylor, Genus Art

Production and printing in England for

STAPLEFORD CENTRE BOOKS

The Stapleford Centre, Stapleford House,
Wesley Place, Stapleford, Nottingham. NG9 8DP.

Registered Office: Stapleford House, Wesley Place, Stapleford, Nottingham NG9 8DP
A company limited by guarantee, registered in England and Wales, number 3371977. Registered Charity number 1063856.

Printed by Progressive Printers, Westbury Road, Basford, Nottingham NG5 1EJ.
Tel. (0115) 970 1485

Layout by Hayman Graphics Tel. (0115) 956 5365

$\mathcal{C}$ontents

$\mathcal{C}$ ontents

ontents

A

All Saints P.15
The meaning of the word 'saint' is explored, emphasising that not all saints are famous or known at all.

St Andrew P.20
An account of what is known about Andrew's life, and the qualities he displayed.

Aotearoa - New Zealand P.60
Some facts about the country. Maori Christian faith and the meaning of the symbol for Christianity.

Ascension P.70
The 'good' and 'bad' news of the Ascension for the disciples. The promise of the Holy Spirit.

B

St. Bathildis P.25
The life of Bathildis, a Saxon saint, is explored, emphasising memories of past hardships reminding people to relieve others' suffering.

Bethany P.84
People's need for relaxation. Mary and Martha's home at Bethany was a place of rest for Jesus: Mary's act of love.

Bethlehem P.83
Bethlehem's connections with Ruth, David and Jesus: a place of rescue.

The Boy from Merthyr P.28
The life of Joseph Parry, a composer of hymn tunes: music as an expression of faith.

John Bunyan 1 P.37 ('The Pilgrim's Progress')
Number one of ten. An introduction to 'The Pilgrim's Progress' assemblies: Bunyan's life.

C

St Catherine P.19
The life and witness of Catherine, an Egyptian martyr in Rome. The origin of the Catherine Wheel.

Christian Loses his Load P.41 ('The Pilgrim's Progress')
Number five of ten. Christian loses his load of guilt caused by the wrong he had done: forgiveness.

Christmas in Kenya P.62
Christmas customs in Kenya. Celebrating Christ born into a world of worry.

Christmas in South India P.63
Christmas customs in South India. Jesus as 'The Light of the World.'

The Circle P.52
The use of symbols: the circle as a symbol of the eternal God.

The City of Destruction P.39 ('The Pilgrim's Progress')
Number three of ten. Life in the City of Destruction: Christian meets Evangelist and sets off on his journey.

A Country called 'Saviour' P.61
Facts about El Salvador. The Salvadorean Christians' battle against poverty and wrong.

A Cup of Tea P.79
A tea-picker's life. The Fair Trade mark: fairness and justice.

D

St David P.21
The life of St David. The use of the dove and leek as symbols connected with his life.

E

Easter Day in Zaire P.69
Easter as a time of celebration: Easter Day customs in Zaire.

Easter in Cyprus P.67
The story of Jesus' death and resurrection. Foods associated with Good Friday and Easter Day. Easter Sunday celebrations in Cyprus.

Easter Sunday: The Orange P.68
The story of Mary Magdalene's meeting with the risen Jesus. Unpleasant and pleasant surprises. Orange-rolling at Dunstable and the reasons for it.

Elizabeth's Story P.49
The birth of John the Baptist.

F

Feeding the 5,000 P.56
The story of the feeding of the 5,000. Jesus' actions are likened to jigsaw pieces, building up a picture of his character.

Fish and Chips P.76
The harvest of the sea: gratitude for it and the dangers of gathering it. The work of the Royal National Mission to Deep Sea Fishermen.

Fortitude P.34 (The Maltese Cross)
Number two of four. Physical strength and inner strength: Joshua as an example of fortitude.

St Francis P.18
The life of Francis: the difference between needing and wanting things.

G

St George P.17
What is known about his life. Fighting 'dragons' today.

Giant Despair P.45 ('The Pilgrim's Progress')
Number nine of ten. Giant Despair and Doubting castle: promise as a key to escape the prison of doubt.

The Giver P.50
The meaning of people's titles in general: the meaning of titles given to God. The story behind the title of 'God the Giver'. Christians' gratitude for the harvest.

God's Builder P.32
The life and work of John Laing the builder, and his promise to God about his use of money.

Good-bye, 'Alleluia' P.65
Giving up things for Lent: why some Christians give up 'Alleluia' at this time.

Good Friday: the Holly P.66

The story of Good Friday: an Easter carol about holly and its meaning.

The Good Newsagent P.85

A modern drama on the parable of the lost sheep, with emphasis on 'the Good Shepherd'.

H

Jane Haining P.30

The life of Jane Haining, a Scottish woman who helped Jewish children in Hungary: our responsibility to others in need.

The Halo P.16

The use of the halo in art to show someone is special to Christians. People in life have no halo to show they are special: how do we know who they are?

The Hand P.53

The hand is one of the symbols used to describe God. The positive uses of our hands. The hand of God as a symbol of his love and care.

Harvest Home P.75

The origin of the Harvest Festival in Britain: Christians' gratitude to God for their food.

Harvest in Tanzania P.73

Difficulties of growing food in Tanzania presented as a game: gratitude for the harvest.

The Heavenly City P.46 ('The Pilgrim's Progress')

Number ten of ten. A description of the Heavenly City and of Heaven: Christian crosses the river.

The Hill of Difficulty P.42 ('The Pilgrim's Progress')

Number six of ten. Christian struggles up the Hill of Difficulty and rests in the Palace Beautiful.

The Human Cost of the Harvest P.81

Where our food comes from: the work of the Missions to Seamen.

J

Justice P.33 (The Maltese Cross)

The first of four. The meaning of justice, and how it is put into practice.

L

The Light of the World P.55

Putting out lights. Sources of light and reflectors of light. Jesus as a source of light and Christians as reflectors of that light. Christians believe Jesus' light was not extinguished.

The Lost Coin P.86

The parable of the lost coin: its background and its meaning. Christians believe that everyone is important to God.

M

MAF P.82
The work of the Mission Aviation Fellowship, whose pilots 'fly to the rescue'.

The Maltese Cross - 4 assemblies, P.33, 34, 35, and 36
These are described under their separate titles: justice, fortitude, temperance and perseverance.

Michal's Trick P.47
The story of Michal tricking her father, Saul, to save her husband David. Difficult decisions.

N

Number 1 P.54
The Christian belief that there is only one God, and that he is first in importance in their lives.

P

St Patrick P.22
The life of Patrick. His return to and work in Ireland, and his opinion of himself.

St Paul P.24
The man who considered hardship worth it.

Pentecost P.71
The difficulty of describing some things. The story of Pentecost and the symbols used to describe the Holy Spirit.

Perseverance P. 36 (The Maltese Cross)
Number four of four. The Christian life as a journey: perseverance is needed to continue with the journey.

St Peter P.23
The life of St Peter: a mixture of success and failure.

'The Pilgrim's Progress' 10 assemblies, P. 37-46
These are described under their separate titles.

The Pound P.77
The level of health care in other countries. What £1 will pay for.

Power from the Sun P.78
The sun's power used in solar ovens, so preventing deforestation: an example of good news, and of science used to help others.

Priest of the Rubbish Tips P.29
The work of Father Samaan and the life of people living on Egypt's rubbish tips. Recycling and our responsibility for others and the planet.

Q

The Quiet Gardens P.80
Our need of peace and quiet. Gardens set aside for this by the Quiet Garden Trust.

R

The Rock P.58
The parable of the two houses. The Church as a rock: action is necessary as well as listening and talking.

Oscar Romero P.27
Ways of silencing people, and Romero's refusal to be silenced.

S

Saying 'Thank you' on the Moon P.72
The meaning of the Eucharist/Communion: Buzz Aldrin celebrates it on the moon.

Helen Sharman P.31
The work of Christian women - in particular that of Helen Sharman, the first British astronaut.

The Ship P.59
The storm on Galilee. The ship as a symbol of the Church. Life as a sea-journey: Christians see Jesus as their captain.

Shrove Tuesday/Bannock Day P.64
The meaning of Shrove Tuesday and Lent for Christians: wrong ingredients in cooking and in life.

The Swamp of Sadness P.40 ('The Pilgrim's Progress')
Number four of ten. Christian is almost lost in the Slough of Despond: promises and Help.

Superparent P.51
The qualities of a superparent: related to God's qualities as reflected in the father in the parable of the prodigal son.

T

Temperance P.35 (The Maltese Cross)
Number three of four. The meaning of temperance: self-control as a sign of strength, not of weakness.

Thanksgiving Day P.74
Thanksgiving Day in America and the reasons for it: gratitude for food.

To be a Pilgrim P.38 ('The Pilgrim's Progress')
Number two of ten. Bunyan's determination to tell others about Jesus even in prison. The 'pilgrim's hymn' and its meaning. An introduction to his use of names.

The Trap P.57
The story of the tribute money, and sketch about Roman taxation in Palestine. Jesus' answer when his enemies tried to trick him: 'deciding what is right and wrong belongs to God, not rulers.'

V

The Valley of Fear ('The Pilgrim's Progress') P.43
Number seven of ten. Christian's encounter with Apollyon, his experience in the Valley of Fear and his meeting with Faithful. This assembly looks at 'fear' monsters.

Vanity Fair P.44 ('The Pilgrim's Progress')
Number eight of ten. The meaning of names explored. Christian is imprisoned in the town of Emptiness. He continues with Hopeful.

W

Waiting for the Light P.48
Waiting for something we want: Simeon and Anna were waiting for Jesus. Candlemas and Jesus as 'The Light of the World.'

Joan Waste of Derby P.26
The life of Joan Waste of Derby: her courage in standing up for her beliefs.

Explaining the title

The assemblies in this book first appeared in the magazine **Cracking RE**, volumes 1-6. This magazine gives practical help on RE and worship to the primary teacher. Each issue contains two topics and twelve assemblies. More information on **Cracking RE** can be found on page 94.

The word assemblies is used in this book simply because that is the term that teachers still use and the term 'act of worship' does not easily roll off the tongue. There is, however, a technical difference between an assembly and an act of worship. Officially an assembly is the notices and the administrative detail. The act of worship is the religious part of the gathering.

Respecting the pupil's integrity

Acts of worship should be appropriate to the family background of the pupils. Respect for the children and their family should be shown. There are several ways of achieving this.

1) The way children are involved in worship should be appropriate. It should be varied in degree as well as the type of participation. Details of different types of participation are given on page 14.

2) The way Christian material is presented. The Christian material in this book should be introduced using phrases such as 'Christians believe'. Assent should not be assumed. This approach protects the integrity of the child and the teacher, whilst enabling a full and accurate presentation of Christianity.

3) The variety of responses which are encouraged. As long as they are respectful, pupils can respond in a variety of ways. Appropriate responses might be anything from simply appreciating that what has been said is important to Christians, right through to adoration of God. Worship should not, indeed it cannot, be compelled. Schools are only required to provide the *opportunity* for worship to take place, no more. In practice this will mean allowing pupils the freedom not to join in certain activities, but to listen quietly instead.

Reflections and prayers

Prayers can be introduced with phrases such as 'I am going to read a Christian Prayer', or 'Listen quietly while the prayer is read. Those who wish to can join in the "amen." ' Alternatively, prayers can be read by pupils. Reflections involve quiet thinking and should be private, open sharing can be intimidating.

Planning ahead

Everyone has to take assemblies at short notice sometimes and to cope with such emergencies teachers have to do 'one off' assemblies. This, however should not be normal practise. Themes should be planned ahead and records kept on a simple proforma. The forms can then be used to create a one year or two year plan. Guidelines for creating your own assemblies can be found on pages 12-14.

Health and Safety

All activities should be conducted with health and safety considerations in mind. Teachers are referred to their Health and Safety document.

Music

If the suggested songs for the assemblies are not appropriate for your school, more general songs can be substituted.

There are a four aspects of an act of worship which need bearing in mind at the planning stage:

Content

Atmosphere

Reflection

Participation

A) Content

The content of a broadly Christian act of worship, can be extremely varied. Below are a few suggestions illustrated by examples from this book.

1) Bible stories (Page 56)
Bible stories can form the basis of an act of worship, but they need rephrasing in a way that makes them accessible to pupils.

2) Poems (Page 15)
Poems are a good source of material, but they have to be the type of poem that will make sense when first heard. The act of worship should not be turned into an English lesson.

3) Non-biblical stories (Page 37-46)
There are traditional tales such as *Babushka* or non biblical stories such as the *Narnia* stories and *The Pilgrims' Progress* which are still within the Christian tradition.

4) Art (Page 43)
Posters, paintings and a variety of works of art can be the focus of an act of worship. One of the problems is finding things large enough to use. Instant art created by the teacher and pupils does not require huge amounts of skill.

5) Drama (Page 85)
This can include mime, sketches, puppets and short plays. Chorus drama requires little preparation and the over head projector works well for shadow puppets.

6) Music (Page 54)
Music can set the atmosphere, be the main content or be part of a reflection. It can involve the pupils in singing, making music or listening. World wide music can introduce pupils to the worship of other communities.

7) Organisations (Page 82)
Children can be introduced to a range of Christian organisations and their work. Many organisations send out information on their work, these leaflets often contain useful information, case studies and biographies.

8) Festivals (Page 62)
Festivals are a popular and natural focus for worship. Sometimes exploring the way a festival is celebrated by a different Christian community can bring new insights.

9)Symbols (Page 52)
Symbols can be a potent way into a subject, as they are simple and direct.

10) Demonstrations (Page 78)
Simple demonstrations of cookery, science, etc. can be very effective and children can often take part.

11) Other countries (Page 67)
Assemblies can be arranged as 'visits' to other countries to find out about them and the life of Christians in those countries.

12) Other Subjects (Page 26)
Subjects such as history can be a rich source of information. For example, characters from the past and past ways of worship can be used.

13) Customs (Page 65)
Customs can prove a useful 'peg' on which to hang ideas. They often can act as a concrete expression of an abstract idea.

14) Everyday things (Page 79)
Worship can spring from the everyday things: from a cup of tea, a leaf, a stone.

15) Biography (Page 30)
Biography need not be a journey from when a person was born until they died. It can be an exploration of what inspired them.

16) Dance (Page 66)

Dance needs preparing beforehand and it should be kept short and simple. It can be a formal dance like a carol or expressive movement to a psalm.

17) Objects (Page 86)

An object can be a focus for the assembly: a lamp, a rucksack, a coin.

18) Places (Page 83)

Biblical places such as Bethany or other places with a religious significance can be a focus for an assembly.

B) Atmosphere

Atmosphere is a crucial part of worship. Just playing different types of music as the pupils enter can affect how they feel. The following factors can affect the atmosphere in an act of worship.

a) the relationships between staff and pupils and the ethos of the school

b) where the assembly takes place, noise and comfort

c) the balance between quiet and talking and the use of music, drama, poetry and art

d) the amount of participation by staff and pupils

e) the balance between a secure environment and discipline and the separation of discipline and administrative issues from worship.

f) the presence of a focus such as a candle, a display or a cloth.

C) Reflection

1) Using music (Page 65)

Music can be played and pupils encouraged to think about it. Music should reflect the subject of an assembly or create a suitable atmosphere for an act of worship.

2) Using sound (Page 86)

Sounds themselves are evocative: money dropping in a tin, a pebble in a pool.

3) Think as you listen (Page 59)

Pupils can be given something specific to think about as they listen to a prayer or reflection.

4) Objects (Page 55)

Objects can be a prayer focus: a candle, a cloth, a piece of string.

5) Reflective poems (Page 36)

Poems for reflection need to be strong on atmosphere rather than purely narrative

6) Written prayers (Page 76)

Prayers can be written by the children or members of staff, or formal written prayers can be used.

7) Responsive prayers (Page 15)

Pupils can participate by joining in responsive prayers or repeating a refrain.

8) Action or 'feely' prayers (Page 23)

Action prayers can involve hand movements or touch. They communicate through the senses.

9) Visual prayers (Page 19)

Visual prayers can be written or drawn. For example the word JUSTICE can be split and written as JUST ICE and a suitable reflection on justice read.

10) Metaphor and simile prayers (Page 46)

Metaphors and similes can be extremely powerful. Life can be likened to a journey, trouble to deep mud and heaven to a city. The mental images can help pupils understand the ideas behind the similies.

D) Participation

Pupils can participate in the following ways:

1) Drama (Page 57)
Pupils can take part in sketches and mime. They can use puppets or form a chorus.

2) Demonstrations (Page 52)
Taking part in experiments and demonstrations can help pupils become part of the activity.

3) Reading poetry/stories/prayers (Page 85)
Pupils can read their own poems stories and prayers and share their work.

4) Responding to prayers (Page 15)
Pupils can join in prayers with actions, responses or a final 'amen'.

5) Music/singing (Page 23)
Percussion can be improvised. Pupils can sing, bring in music and play their own instruments.

6) Answering questions (Page 17)
Making their own suggestions and answering questions involves pupils, but questions should be genuine and pupil answers/suggestions need sensitive handling.

7) Instant art (Page 43)
Pupils respond well to art and enjoy making things as part of an assembly.

9) Creating displays (Page 37)
Displays can be created over a number of days and they can hold a theme together. Pupils can bring in items to add to the display.

10) Dance (Page 53)
Pupils can prepare dance or movement to interpret music, poetry or a reading.

You will need

Sock or stamps (for older pupils)
A certificate, cup and a badge (for younger pupils)
Paper and pen

Introduction

When someone is publicly recognised as a saint, some Christians put the letters St. (short for saint) before that person's name - for example: St. David, St. Catherine, St. George. The poet Candia McWilliam has had some fun with this idea making up impossible saints for all sorts of things. Pupils might like to make up a few of their own using words beginning with St. For example: St. Ick the saint for glue, St. Ain (the saint of mess), St. Air (for steps), St. Op (for ending things). Read the poem and use as many items to illustrate it as possible. You will need to write up the first word of each line.

St. Ocking is the saint for socks
St. Ar for deep black night
St. Icking plaster for after shocks
St. Ew for a tough old bite
St. Ickle backs the man for stings,
St. Alagmites for drips,
St. Amp for postage, sending things,
St. Eak goes well with chips.

ST. ICKING

Alternative introduction for younger children

If we achieve at something we sometimes get a certificate or a cup or a badge (show some of these items). Some people have the word 'saint' put in front of their name. It shows they have achieved, not at swimming or football, not at writing or maths, but at living as a Christian.

Core material

Who are these people who have the word saint before their name? Can just anyone be a saint?

The answer is yes and no. In the Bible, the word 'saint' refers to a Christian. It is just another way of saying 'someone who follows Jesus.' There is also another way of using the word 'saint'. In some churches, certain people are recognised as extra special. That might be because they died for their faith, or they lived a particularly outstanding Christian life, or God worked through them in a special way. These people are often publicly recognised as 'saints' and have the word 'saint' put before their name.

That does not mean that people who do not have the word 'saint' before their name are not important or appreciated. There are many people whom we will never know about, who have bravely kept their beliefs under difficult circumstances. Although we may not know them, Christians believe God does.

Prayer/Reflection

Ask pupils to think about some of the special people they may have heard about, people who are special because of the way they lived, not because they are rich or famous. If appropriate, they can join in the prayer by repeating 'We thank you Heavenly Father.'

For all the special people of God - We thank you, Heavenly Father.
For all the examples of love and faith - We thank you, Heavenly Father.
For the known and the unknown saints who make this life richer - We thank you, Heavenly Father.

Music suggestions

'I sing a song of the saints of God.' A Time to Sing, ed. H. Clarke and P. Kneale (Macmillan 1990)
'People who help.' Rejoice 1, comp. A. White, A. Byrne, C. Malone (Harper Collins Religious 1993)

Poem taken from 'Casting a Spell' compiled by Angela Huth. Orchard Publishing 1991. Reproduced with permission.

You will need

Gold tinsel
Gold or yellow paper
Some dressing up clothes
Scissors and sellotape
A large sheet of red paper

Introduction

If you wanted to show that someone was very special, how would you do it?

Ask pupils for their suggestions. If possible, use one pupil to demonstrate.

You might dress them in rich and beautiful clothes. (Use the dressing up clothes.)

You might put a crown on them.
(Make a gold or yellow paper crown)

You might roll out a red carpet for them to stand on. (Stand them on red paper.)

Core material

When artists drew Christians who were extra special, they often drew a halo around their head. A halo is a circle of light. It looks like a circle of gold. It is not really there - special people do not walk around with a gold circle on their heads in real life. It was an artist's way of saying, 'This person is very special.'

Some of you may have worn a halo if you played an angel in the school nativity play. Demonstrate a halo with the tinsel. With older children teachers might like to explore common uses of the word, 'Your halo's slipped' or 'Polish your halo'. When you see a painting and you see a person with a gold circle around their head, remember it is the artist telling you this is someone extra special to Christians. They might be special because they are a character from the Bible. They might be special because of what they did in their life. They might be people who stood firm for their faith in difficult circumstances, or obeyed God when it was hard to do so.

There are many people who are special in this way. We cannot spot them because they do not walk around with halos on. We know them by the way they live: by their courage, gentleness and goodness.

Prayer/Reflection

Ask pupils to think about people who they think are very special. The prayer below can be read.

Thank you Father for all the special people who walk the earth making it a better place.

They may look ordinary, they may not wear halos, but you know all about them.

You see the lives they lead, and the good they do.

Music suggestions

'This little light of mine.' Come and Praise Beginning, comp. G. Marshall-Taylor and D. Coombes (BBC 1996)

'Lord, make me a mountain.' Junior Praise 2, comp. P. Burt, P. Horrobin and G. Leavers (Marshall Pickering 1992)

Biblical material
Isaiah 41.10

'Do not be afraid, for I am with you....I will make you strong and will help you.'

You will need
An outline drawing of a dragon - enlarge the one supplied

Introduction
What does it mean to be brave? Ask pupils for their suggestions. A brave person is someone who faces up to something that is frightening them. It might be a visit to the hospital, or a test at school, going to bed in the dark, or meeting someone who has been nasty to us. We cannot be really brave unless we are frightened to begin with. It isn't brave to jump off the horse in the gym lesson unless jumping off it frightens us! Of course, it is sensible to be frightened of some things. Some things are dangerous - like fire and traffic. We would be silly to say we were not afraid of these things: we have to be careful when we are near them. Some people are called heroes because they face up to the things that frighten them so that they can help other people. Fire fighters do not risk their lives to prove they are brave, but to save other people, and then they are as careful as they can be. Today (or April 23rd) is St George's Day, when we remember St George and what he did. But no one is completely sure what he did do!

Core material
The traditional story tells of George arriving at a small village in the hills. He soon saw that everyone was very unhappy, and frightened. He asked what was happening, and someone explained that a great dragon had come to live nearby. Every day, the monster attacked the village, and many of the people had been killed. George prayed to God. He was frightened at the thought of attacking this dragon, but he knew that he must try to kill it. He asked God to help him to be brave and to make him strong enough to kill the beast. And, with God's help, he managed to kill it.

No one is very sure when George lived, but we think that he was a soldier in the Roman army in the days when the Romans ruled over many different countries. We do know that he was a Christian.

For many years the word 'dragon' was a symbol of evil. The story of St George could be like a parable about defeating evil. George may have fought the evil 'dragon' of hatred and persecution.

How many of you have met a dragon? We have never seen one, but we do meet a sort of 'dragon' every day, because we meet 'dragons' of wrong. George's 'dragon' was probably 'hatred'. Greed, lies and violence can all be 'dragons' we meet in daily life. Ask children for suggestions of other 'dragons' and write them in the outline of the dragon. Christians believe George was brave enough to face his 'dragon' and strong enough to defeat it, because he asked God to help him. Christians believe that people today can ask God for help, too, when they have to face things that frighten them.

Prayer/Reflection
Ask pupils to think about one thing on the 'dragon' and /or read the prayer.

Father, Thank you for people like George who are brave when they are frightened so that they can help other people. Help us to remember that we can ask you to help us to be brave, when we face our dragons.

Music suggestions
'April 23rd is here.' Big Blue Planet, ed. J. Jarvis (Stainer and Bell Ltd. and Methodist Church Division of Education and Youth 1995)

'When a knight won his spurs.' The Complete Come and Praise, comp. G. Marshall-Taylor (BBC 1990)

Biblical material
Philippians 3.8

I believe everything else to be worthless compared with the great richness of knowing Jesus.

You will need
Examples or pictures of pairs of things such as :

  a large bar of chocolate and a loaf of bread
  a pair of shoes and a pair of 'designer' trainers

Introduction
Hold up each article in turn and ask who wants it. Then hold each up and asks who needs it. Bring out the difference between the two words, 'wants' and 'needs'. On October 4th, people remember a man who lived hundreds of years ago who learned this difference. Francis lived in Assisi, a small Italian town on top of a hill. There are many stories told about his friendship with animals: and this is what most people remember him for. But this was not what he was famous for during his life.

Core material
Francis' father was a very rich man! So Francis always had whatever he wanted as he was growing up. But then things went wrong. He became a soldier, and was captured and held prisoner. After that he was very ill. When he finally returned to Assisi, he realised that he was not really happy. It did not seem right for him to have so much when so many people were short of things like food.

One day in church, Francis became certain that God wanted him to work for him. His father was not pleased when he found out. He had wanted Francis to take over his trade after him. But Francis told him, 'I must obey God. This is all I want to do.' He said that he was going to marry Lady Poverty. Poverty means poorness. He didn't mean that he had really found someone called Lady Poorness! He meant that he was going to leave all his riches and wealth behind and live very simply. To show that he meant what he said, he took off the beautiful comfortable clothes he was wearing.

From then on, he relied on what people gave him for his food and his clothes and his shelter. He believed that God would make sure he had whatever he needed to continue his work for him. Many people followed Francis when they saw how he loved God. He became known as 'the poor man'. But he was happy. He agreed with what another follower of God had said years before. Read the biblical material. He had learned that there is a difference between wanting something and needing something.

Prayer/Reflection
This is part of a prayer: we do not know who wrote it.

*'I asked for strength - and God gave me difficulties to make me strong.
I asked for wealth - and God gave me a brain and a body to work with.
I asked for love - and God gave me people in need whom I could love.
I received nothing I wanted.
But I received everything I needed!'*

Music suggestions
'The song of St Francis'. The Complete Come and Praise, comp. G. Marshall-Taylor (BBC 1990)
'One, two, three and four.' Come and Praise Beginning, comp. G. Marshall-Taylor and D. Combes (BBC 1996)

Biblical material

I Peter 3.15-16

Always be prepared to explain what you believe and give a reason for your hope when someone asks you, but do it with gentleness.

You will need

A drawing of a Catherine Wheel firework (provided)
A piece of lace

Introduction

Show the drawing of the firework (Catherine Wheel) and spend time talking about safety for bonfire night. Ask the pupils how much they can remember of the firework code.

Although bonfire night is a time for fun and laughter, there is one firework which is a reminder of more serious things. Show the drawing of the Catherine Wheel. Explain that it is named after St Catherine. St Catherine's Day is November 25th, but many people are reminded of her on November 5th because of the Catherine Wheel firework.

Core material

In the year 305, the Roman Emperor Maxentius captured many people from the town of Alexandria in Egypt. He took the people he had captured to Rome as prisoners. Among the prisoners was an eighteen year old girl called Catherine. Catherine was a Christian and she was both beautiful and intelligent. The Emperor wanted to marry her, but she refused. He also tried to force her to give up her Christian faith. Maxentius tried argument. He got many scholars to try and convince Catherine that it was foolish to be a Christian, but Catherine was able to give reasons for her faith in God.

After that the Emperor tried threatening her, but Catherine still would not give up her faith. Finally, the Emperor had her thrown in a dungeon. Even in prison

Catherine stood up for her beliefs, so the Emperor decided that if he could not bully her into changing her mind, she would have to die. Catherine was condemned to die on a wheel but when the day of her execution came, the wheel broke. Although Catherine was executed eventually, she is remembered as a saint who stood up for what she believed, against someone who tried to bully her into changing her mind. The firework, the Catherine Wheel, is named after her. St Catherine's Day is just before the start of Advent. Advent used to be a very serious time, like Lent. Many years ago you could not get married in Advent, so St Catherine's Day became popular for weddings as it was just before Advent.

The wheel upon which Catherine was meant to die not only gave its name to a firework, it also reminded people of a spinning wheel, and Catherine became the patron saint of spinners and lace makers (show the lace).

Prayer/Reflection

A Catherine Wheel prayer. This prayer can be copied onto an overhead projector acetate, enlarged on the photocopier or copied on a large sheet of paper and put on display as a visual prayer. Ask the pupils to look at the wheel while you read the verse around the rim and some of the qualities of Catherine on the spokes. Pupils can spend a few moments in silence reflecting on these.

Music suggestions

'Stand up, stand up for Jesus.' Junior Praise, comp. by P. Horrobin and G. Leavers (Marshall Pickering 1986)

'Stand firm.' Many and Great, ed. J. L. Bell (Wild Goose Publications 1990)

Biblical material

One day Andrew and a friend were listening to John the Baptist when John suddenly pointed to Jesus and said, ' Look! Here is the one God has sent to take away the sins of the world.' Andrew and his friend followed after Jesus and spent the day with him. In the afternoon, Andrew went to find his brother Simon. 'Come quickly, Simon,' said Andrew. 'I've found the special King God promised.' Simon looked up wondering what Andrew was talking about. Reluctantly he went with him to see Jesus. Jesus smiled when he saw Simon. 'You are Simon,' he said. 'But you shall be Peter, the rock.' *John 1.35-42*

Some time later, Jesus was walking by the Sea of Galilee when he saw Simon and Andrew fishing with their nets. 'Come follow me,' said Jesus. 'I will make you fishers of men.' Simon and Andrew left their nets and followed Jesus. *Mark 1.16-20*

Jesus spoke to a great crowd of people, over five thousand of them. It grew late and the people were hungry. 'Where shall we find bread to feed all these people?' asked Philip. 'Even if we could find enough bread it would cost too much, for we do not have much money.' Andrew spoke up. 'I know it won't go round all these people,' he said. 'But I've found a boy with five barley loaves and two fish.' For Jesus it was enough: he made the people sit down. He blessed the bread, and those five loaves and two fish fed all the people. *John 6.1-13*

One day some people from Greece came to see Jesus. They went first of all to Philip to ask if they could see him. 'Sir,' they said. 'We want to see Jesus.' Philip told Andrew and Andrew told Jesus. *John 12.20-22*

You will need

Blue paper, white paper
A large felt-tipped-pen
Scissors
Sticky-Tak

Introduction

Ask what special day it is and how many people are called Andrew/ Andrea. Make a cross of St Andrew using a piece of blue paper and two white strips and ask which country it signifies. St Andrew is the patron saint of Scotland. The Scottish flag is blue with a white diagonal cross.

Core material

Andrew was a fisherman who followed Jesus. He was Jesus' first named disciple. We do not know for certain what happened to him after Jesus' death. He is thought to have taken the Christian message to Russia, probably dying there in about 60AD. It is said he was crucified on a diagonal cross. The cross of St Andrew is the national flag of Scotland and also makes up part of the Union flag. If you have a Union flag, ask pupils to find St Andrew's cross on it. Andrew's symbol is the white diagonal cross on a blue background (the sea) or a fishing net. Ask pupils why they think these symbols were chosen.

There are various legends linking Andrew and Scotland. One says that St Regulus brought some of his bones to Scotland and housed them in a church where St Andrews now stands. Another story maintains that the diagonal cross of St Andrew shone in the sky when the Picts were fighting the English. It is more likely that the association with Andrew is the result of St Acca meeting King Angus MacFergus and giving (or selling) him some of the relics of St Andrew which he had brought back from Rome.

Read the biblical stories about Andrew. After each one ask pupils what it tells us about Andrew's character. Write the suggestions inside the white diagonals (see illustration). There is not a lot of information about Andrew but what we have gives us a clue as to the type of person he was.

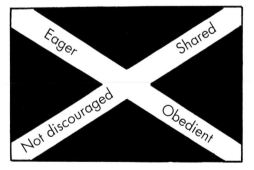

Prayer/Reflection

Ask pupils to look at the flag and think about those qualities in their own lives.

Music suggestions

'A boy gave to Jesus.' Junior Praise comp. P. Horrobin and G. Leavers (Marshall Pickering 1986)

'March the first is here again.' (verse for St Andrew) Big, Blue Planet, ed. J. Jarvis (Stainer and Bell Ltd and Methodist Church Division of Education and Youth 1995)

You will need

A leek
Enlarged photocopies of the dove and the other signs

Introduction

Introduce the idea of signs and symbols. Start by showing some signs. The ones provided can be enlarged on the photocopier and used. Pupils may be able to suggest or draw other signs.

Signs

No Smoking   No bicycles

Signs give directions and information in a simple form. A symbol is a sign which evokes (causes) a response (feeling). A cross evokes a response from a Christian - it gives more than information. A dove means peace and indicates the presence of God the Holy Spirit (see below).

Symbols

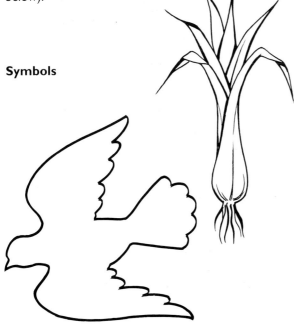

Core material

Hold up the leek. Ask what it is. If you are not Welsh, the leek is just a vegetable. If someone holds one up, you might feel hungry if you like leeks and hope you have them for dinner. If you don't like leeks, you might decide to have tea at a friend's that night! If you are Welsh, the leek creates a feeling of pride as it is a symbol of Wales and St David. The leek was worn by Welsh soldiers when in battle, to enable them to recognise each other. The idea of using a leek came from St David.

David was born in Henfynyw (henn-vunue) in Cardigan, Wales. He became a monk and later founded many monasteries, the most well known being at Mynyw (mun-ue), today known as St David's. David and his monks spread the Christian message throughout Wales. There are various symbols associated with St David: the leek is only one of them. Many of the stories associated with David involve a dove, the symbol of the Holy Spirit, which is the name Christians give to God, present and active. The Holy Spirit is like a real, but invisible friend. Drawing the symbol of a dove for David is a way of saying that God was with David, helping him and guiding him.

Prayer/Reflection

Read the Christian prayer or ask pupils to think about people like David who give their lives to spreading a message of love and forgiveness.

As you were with David, be with us, Lord.
As the symbol of the leek reminds people of David and Wales,
So may the symbol of the dove remind people you are close.

Music suggestions

'Mis Mawrth Unwaith Eto' / 'March the first is here again.' Big Blue Planet, ed. J. Jarvis (Stainer and Bell Ltd and Methodist Church Division of Education and Youth 1995)

'I've got peace like a river.' Junior Praise, comp. by P. Horrobin and G. Leavers (Marshall Pickering 1986)

You will need

A selection of clean stones
One stone with mud or earth on it

Introduction

Talk about the way walls are built from stones. Walls made from dry stones have no cement to hold them, the stones are carefully selected for size and shape and fitted together to make a wall. Specially shaped stones are arranged along the top, as in the diagram. Show the stones (not the muddy one) to pupils and ask them to select stones they would use for building a wall.

Core material

Patrick was a young Christian teenager who lived on the coast of Britain in the fifth Century. One day, Irish raiders landed and captured him. Patrick was taken to Ireland where he worked as a slave on a farm looking after animals. It was a far cry from the comfortable home he had experienced in Britain. He must have felt terribly alone in a strange land where the people spoke a different language and had a different religion. For six years Patrick worked as a slave, and during that time his faith, which he had learnt in a Christian home, became very real to him. Patrick prayed while he looked after the animals and felt that God was looking after him.

After six years of slavery, Patrick escaped and eventually made his way back to Britain. His family must have been pleased to see him after so many years! Patrick's quiet life was short-lived, however. Once again it was the Irish who disturbed his peaceful existence, but in a very different way. Patrick dreamed he heard a voice calling him: it was the voice of the Irish calling him back, asking him to come and work among them. Patrick was reluctant to leave, but he knew that God was calling him to share the message of Jesus in Ireland. The Irish were not strangers now. He understood their language and he knew the land and the people. In 432, Patrick and some friends landed in Ireland and for the rest of his life he shared the Christian message with the Irish people, eventually dying in Ireland in about 460.

Patrick described himself as a muddy stone (show the stone) that God had picked from a ditch and placed on top of a wall. In other words, he was very ordinary. Any greatness he had achieved (being on top of the wall) was achieved through the strength of God.

Prayer/Reflection

Ask pupils to look at the stone while you read the extract from the hymn by T.A.B. Smyth. Or think about Ireland today and its need for peace and reconciliation.

For Saint Patrick's youthful vision,
For the call he clearly heard,
Lord, we thank you and remember
His obedience to your word.
(Adapted)

Music suggestions

'March the first is here again.' (verse for St. Patrick). Big Blue Planet ed J. Jarvis (Stainer and Bell Ltd and Methodist Church Division of Education and Youth 1995)

'Prayer of Saint Patrick.' A Year of Celebration ed. J. Porter and J. McCrimmon (McCrimmons 1995)

Note: A leaflet on Patrick is available from The Learning Resources Unit, Stranmillis College, Belfast BT9 5DY.

Introduction

Mark burst into the kitchen. 'Had a good day at school?' asked his Mum.

'Well - yes and no,' he replied.

Mum sat down. 'What do you mean by that?' she asked.

'I started off well,' Mark explained. 'I was the only one who had found out about kangaroos last night, so Miss Spencewell was pleased with me. But then I argued with her about how to load the new programme on the computer - and she was right all along anyway! Then I tidied up for her after painting - even though it wasn't my turn.'

'That was good, at least, then,' said Mum.

'Yes - but then I threw a football and spilt all the paint on the floor.'

'Oh dear! Not so good, then, Mark,' Mum decided.

'No, and it got worse. That new boy - Stephen - hit Terry. I saw him do it, but when Miss Spencewell asked if anyone had seen what happened, I was too frightened to tell her that I'd seen him. But then, later on, I went to see her by myself and told her - and she was pleased. She understood why I hadn't said anything earlier on, so the day didn't end too badly after all.'

Core material

Do you ever have days like that? You start off determined to do everything right, but other things and people get in the way, and even the things you do yourself go wrong. Peter, one of Jesus' disciples, knew just what this was like - his whole life was a mixture of successes and failures. Show the pupils how to make 'thumbs up' and 'thumbs down' signs, and discuss their meanings. Originally the Roman Emperor gave either the thumbs up or down sign, signifying whether a man should live or die in the arena. Today it just means 'OK' or 'not OK'. Read these short accounts of some of the events of Peter's life, and ask them to decide which sign to give (silently) at the end of each.

1. When Jesus asked Peter to follow him, Peter went with him straightaway.

2. Once, Jesus walked on the water towards the disciples while they were in a boat. Peter wanted to join him, and he climbed out of the boat - and walked on the water as well, with Jesus' help.

3. But when he looked at the rough waves, he forgot that Jesus was helping him and he began to sink!

4. Jesus asked the disciples whom they thought he was. Several of them were not sure, but Peter said, 'God's special King, the Messiah.' Jesus was very pleased when he heard this. He said, 'God must have told you this, Peter.'

5. Jesus sometimes chose just three of his disciples to see and hear things that the others did not see or hear. Peter was one of these three.

6. When Jesus knew that he would soon die, he warned the disciples that they would soon be so frightened that they would all abandon him. Peter said, 'I will never leave you, Jesus!'

7. But when Jesus was arrested, Peter was so frightened that he told people he had never even met Jesus.

8. After Jesus rose from death, he asked Peter to lead his followers and to teach them and look after them. Peter realised that Jesus had forgiven him.

9. Peter became an important leader of the church. He was often imprisoned and punished because he taught about Jesus, but he said, 'I have to teach other people about Jesus and his love for them - whatever happens to me.'

Prayer/Reflection

Ask pupils to make the 'thumbs down' sign and think about times when, no matter how hard they tried, things went wrong. Now ask them to make the 'thumbs up' sign and think of times when they have struggled to do their best and things have gone well.

Music suggestions

'Father, hear the prayer we offer.' The Complete Come and Praise, comp. G. Marshall-Taylor (BBC 1990)

'Every day if you go astray.' Junior Praise 2, comp. P. Burt, P. Horrobin and G. Leavers (Marshall Pickering 1992)

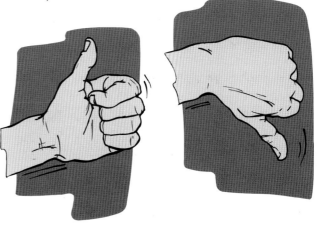

You will need

A pair of balance scales and some small slips of paper to 'weigh'

Introduction

Ask the pupils to close their eyes and to think about what they did on each day of the last week. Did any of them do anything they really enjoyed? Did any of them have annoying or difficult days during the week? (Do not ask for details of any of these.)

We often hear people saying things such as, 'I've had a good day', or 'I've had a difficult day!' What might happen on a 'good' day? Write their suggestions on slips of paper. Do the same for an 'annoying or difficult' day. Show them the scales. If you collected the 'good' things on one side and the 'annoying/difficult' things on the other, how would you know what sort of day that person had had? Talk about one side outweighing the other.

Core material

Paul was one of the leaders of Jesus' followers in the years when the Church was just beginning. He spent many years travelling around different countries to tell people about Jesus and about his love for them. This work was often difficult and dangerous. Many people wanted to stop him doing it. Later, Paul spent some time looking back over his whole life. He thought about things that had been 'good' or 'difficult' in his life, as we have just done. Here is what he said about his life:

'As I travelled, I was often in great danger. Some people were determined to stop me. Many times I really thought that I was about to be killed. But this danger just made me trust God even more. People have said terrible and cruel things to me. They have called me a liar, and said I was just tricking others by my lies. I have had to work very hard, because I have often had to earn enough money for food as well as spending so much time teaching people. Even so, I have often been very hungry! I have had some terrifying sea-journeys. In fact, I have been ship-wrecked three times. Once, I was adrift in the sea for a whole night and day before I was rescued! People have whipped me and beaten me. I have spent long hours in prison, and I have nearly been stoned to death. In some towns, I have been caught up in riots which nearly killed me. Many people have wanted to see me killed. But, in all of these difficulties, I have known that I had

the most important things of all. I have known that God loved me, and I have known that I have been doing my best to obey him. These things are far more important than all the terrible things that have happened to me.' *(taken from a number of Paul's letters)*

Ask the pupils for the 'good' things and the 'difficult' things in Paul's life, and write them on the slips of paper. As you work, ask on which side each slip belongs, and put them in the scales. At the end, show which side has more slips of paper. According to this list, what sort of life did Paul have? But he did not see it like this. Re-read the last two sentences about his life. He said that, however he had suffered, he was still happy when he looked back on his life, because he knew that God loved him and that he had done what God wanted him to do.

Prayer/Reflection

A pupil might like to read the prayer below.
Sometimes we have good days, when everything seems fine.
Sometimes we have difficult days, when everything seems to go wrong.
Whatever the day is like, God's love is still there.

Music suggestions

'Through all the changing scenes of life.' Junior Praise 1, comp. P. Horrobin and G. Leavers (Marshall Pickering 1986)

'Jesus' love is very wonderful.' Jump Up if You're Wearing Red! (National Society/Church House Publishing 1996)

You will need
Some photographs

Introduction
Ask pupils how we remember things that happened a long time ago.

Photographs are one way of remembering. We can look back at past events and be reminded of things that happened a long time ago. Show some photographs and if the pupils have brought any in, ask them to talk about their photographs. If you have a Polaroid camera you can take photographs in the assembly.

Core material
Today's story is about a saint who never forgot. Bathildis was a poor English girl. She had an eventful life. As a young girl, she was captured by pirates and sold as a slave to a man who worked for the King of France. The King of France was so impressed by Bathildis that he married her. Bathildis had three sons, each of whom became King of France after their father.

Bathildis herself never forgot what it was like to be poor and to be a slave. She spent her whole life building hospitals, freeing slaves, and selling her own jewellery to help those in need.

Bathildis did not have photographs to remind her, she had to rely on her memory. She remembered those terrible days of poverty, then being captured by pirates and being sold as a slave. These events must have been so deeply engraved in her mind that she did not need photographs. If possible, enlarge the 'photographs' of the life of Bathildis to illustrate this point.

Every time Bathildis saw someone in need, it reminded

her of what it was like to be poor and hungry. Every time she saw a slave, it reminded her of what it was like to be sold. Her memories moved her to action.

Prayer/Reflection
Ask pupils to think about times when they have seen people lonely or upset. If they have experienced a similar situation, did this help them understand how the people felt? Bathildis used her memories for good.

Music suggestions
'Make me a channel of your peace.' Alleluya, comp. D. Gadsby and J. Hogarth (A and C Black 1980)

'Care for one another.' Children's Praise, comp. P. Burt, P. Horrobin and G. Leavers (Marshall Pickering 1991)

You will need

A blindfold
A packet of cornflakes
Milk in a jug
A bowl and spoon

Introduction

Ask pupils to do a number of simple, but safe, tasks blindfolded. Ask a blindfolded member of staff to pour and eat a bowl of cornflakes. When it is an activity for a few minutes, eating or doing tasks blindfolded can seem fun. When this is reality, and for life, it is anything but fun. A blindfold is also an inaccurate way of experiencing blindness, even for a few moments, for we still have the memory of what things look like in our 'mind's eye.' Imagine what it would be like if you had never seen these things. (This will need handling very sensitively). Today's story is about a woman who had been blind from birth. She lived over four hundred years ago.

Core material

Joan was born in the reign of Henry VIII. She was the daughter of William Waste, a barber and rope maker from Derby. Although blind from birth, Joan learned to knit and sew, and she also helped her father make ropes. When her parents died, Joan went to live with her twin brother Roger.

Joan had a strong Christian faith and daily attended church. Without anyone to guide her, she was able to find her way to any of the churches in Derby. She also had a tremendous memory and memorised large amounts of the Bible. Joan always wanted a Bible of her own, and saved up to buy a New Testament. She persuaded a friend called John Hurt to read it to her. John was over seventy and was imprisoned for debt, so Joan used to visit the prison and he would read to her. When John Hurt could not read to her, Joan asked the parish clerk, John Pemberton, to read instead. If neither John could read, she paid people a few pence to do so.

Life continued like this until 1553 when Queen Mary came to the throne, then life changed dramatically for Joan. Like many other Protestants, she refused to give up her faith and was imprisoned. Joan was brought to trial in All Saints' Church (now Derby Cathedral) but she refused to change her mind. On August 1st 1556, Joan was executed - one of the many ordinary men and women who died for their faith.

Note: this will link with the Tudors in History. The story needs careful handling. During this period both Catholics and Protestants died for their beliefs. The emphasis should be on the courage of Joan Waste in standing up for what she believed.

Prayer/Reflection

In Birchover Church, there is a memorial to Joan Waste which reads:

She was poor, yet made many rich;
ignorant, yet a match for the scholars of the day:
born blind, yet she had a clear vision of God's truth,
young, 22, yet wiser than the aged;
homeless yet with a place in heaven.

Music suggestions

'My faith it is an oaken staff.' The Complete Come and Praise, comp. G. Marshall-Taylor (BBC 1990)

'When you're in a jam.' Children's Praise, comp. P. Burt, P. Horrobin and G. Leavers (Marshall Pickering 1991)

Biblical material
Psalm 35.10; 140.12

There is no one like you, God. You look after the weak and protect the poor against the bully. God defends the cause of the poor and stands up for the rights of the needy.

You will need
A teacher with a book

Introduction
Arrange for a member of staff to read from a book and not to stop whatever happens. It doesn't matter what he/she reads. Ask pupils to suggest ways of stopping him/her talking. Demonstrate these.

You could ask her to be quiet.
You could tell her to be quiet.
You could threaten her to make her quiet.
You could force her to be quiet. (Put a hand over her mouth - gently.)

Core material
Oscar Romero was a quiet, shy man. He became Archbishop (Christian leader) of a country called El Salvador in Central America. Many people thought he would stay quiet because he was shy and timid. Read the pupils some facts about El Salvador to give them some background (page 92).

Despite his shyness, Oscar Romero began to speak out about the wrongs in his country. He spoke out about the poverty, the violence and injustice. He not only spoke, he acted. He said that his words were a voice for the people. Some people tried to shut him

up. He was asked, he was told, and finally he was threatened, but quiet, shy Oscar Romero kept speaking. The government began to worry. People were listening to the Archbishop, and the poor people loved him. Romero knew his life was in danger, but he kept speaking up for the poor. He knew someone might try to shut him up permanently by killing him, but he said this: 'I have often been threatened with death....I have to say this, I do not believe in death without resurrection: if I die, I will rise again in the Salvadorean people.' In 1980, Oscar Romero was shot. He had been right. There was not a silence after his death. Other Christians followed his example and spoke and acted on behalf of the poor of El Salvador.

Prayer/Reflection
Ask pupils to think about times they have spoken up for others. Read the extract from the prayer from Central America. Explain that it is written by Christians who live in situations like that of El Salvador.

'Forgive us for keeping silent in the face of injustice and for burying our dreams.'

Music suggestions
This song is based on one sung in El Salvador and can be learnt by the pupils if appropriate.

Song arranged by Helen Johnson (Out of the Ark Music)
Prayer taken from 'A Generous Land' published by Cafod, Christian Aid, SCIAF, Trocaire. Available from these organisations. See page 92.

Holy, Holy, Holy Is The Lord

El Salvador

1. Ho - ly, ho - ly, ho - ly, ho - ly,___ ho - ly, ho - ly is our God. God the Lord of earth and
2. Ho - ly, ho - ly, ho - ly, ho - ly,___ ho - ly, ho - ly is our God. God the Lord of ev' - ry

heav - en, ho - ly, ho - ly is our God. Ho - ly, ho - ly, ho - ly, ho - ly,___ ho - ly,
na - - tion,___ ho - ly, ho - ly is our God. Ho - ly, ho - ly, ho - ly, ho - ly,___ ho - ly,

ho - ly is our God, God the Lord of all of his - tory,___ ho - ly, ho - ly is our God.
ho - ly is our God, God who walks be - side our peo - ple,___ ho - ly, ho - ly is our God.

You will need
Someone who can play the piano (optional)
Paper and pencil
Recording of the theme tune from 'Top of the Pops' (optional)

Introduction
If possible, record the theme tune of 'Top of the Pops' to start this assembly. Ask pupils for their favourite songs out of the ones that they sing in assembly. Try to create a top 'ten'. (Use only about five - ten takes too long!) You will need several staff to help you with this as it will involve a rough count.

Alternatively, have a basic clapometer. This can be made with a piece of card. Draw a calibrated circle on the card and use a butterfly clip to attach a 'hand'. The 'hand' can be moved manually in response to the clapping. Accuracy is not vitally important!

Ask the person playing the piano to play a little of each of five popular assembly songs, or if you do not have a pianist, the pupils can just name them. Children can clap after each one. Talk about the way music can help people express their feelings and beliefs.

Core material
Joseph Parry was born in the Welsh town of Merthyr Tydfil in 1841. At the age of nine, Joseph began working down a coal mine for twelve hours each day. For that work, he earned 5 pennies (old money) a day (about 2p). Later, when he was twelve, Joseph went to work at the iron works. Joseph's mother was very musical and Joseph himself sang in the chapel choir. Life was very hard for the Parry family. Eventually, the family emigrated to America and settled down in Pennsylvania. Joseph worked in the steel mills. He had a good voice but he could not read a note of music. Working next to him in the mill was a man called John Abel Jones. John could read music and he gave Joseph music lessons after work. Joseph loved learning. He pestered John Abel Jones so that he could learn as much as possible.

Joseph began to compose his own music. In 1865, he returned to Wales, and friends there raised enough money to send him to music college. Joseph completed college and became very successful. He wrote music so fast they used to call him 'the lightning composer.' Joseph did his

best to write a new hymn tune every week for church. 'Aberystwyth' is his best known hymn tune. When Joseph Parry died in 1903, 7,000 sang to that tune at his funeral service. He had given Christians, all over Wales and far beyond, the music with which to express their faith.

Prayer/Reflection
If possible, listen to 'Aberystwyth' being played. The hymn that is often sung to this tune describes trouble as a storm, and running to hide in Jesus' arms until the storm is over. The music is sad and solemn for it describes a sad situation. It is also very strong music. Christians believe Jesus is strong and comforts people in trouble. Alternatively, pupils can listen to any suitable music while they say 'thank you' silently for the gift of music.

Note: the music 'Aberystwyth' can be found in most traditional hymn books. It is often used for the hymn 'Jesu, lover of my soul'.

Music suggestions
'Maybe you can't draw or sing.' Junior Praise 2, comp. P. Burt, P. Horrobin and G. Leavers (Marshall Pickering 1992)

'Hey, now, everybody sing!' Alleluya, comp. D. Gadsby and J. Hogarth (A and C Black 1980)

Biblical material

Genesis 2.8, 9, 15

God planted a garden called Eden and there he placed the man he had made. All kinds of beautiful trees grew there and produced fruit....He put man in the garden to look after it and guard it carefully.

You will need

A plastic rubbish bag containing safe items of rubbish which could have been recycled

Introduction

Show your bag of rubbish and ask the pupils how the items could have been recycled rather than thrown away. Talk about waste with the pupils and the need to recycle. For Christians, recycling is part of looking after the world. They imagine the earth as God's garden and the people as his gardeners. Read the biblical material. Although this talks of a particular garden, Eden, the word Eden means 'delight' and Christians sometimes think of the whole earth as God's garden because they see the whole world as 'delightful'. If we do not recycle, material will run out or we will use more and more energy in creating more goods.

Core material

Father Samaan is a Christian priest from Cairo in Egypt. Father Samaan became friends with the man who collected his rubbish. Eventually he went to visit his friend and found that he lived, along with many others, in a house made of oil drums on a hill covered in rubbish. Twenty thousand people make a living from recycling the rubbish in Egypt. Here is the story of Father Samaan's friend, Joe.

Joe's Day

Joe, who is thirteen, has a brother John and a sister

Samah. His family collect and recycle rubbish in Cairo. This is his diary for a normal day. NOTE: Teachers might like to compare Joe's day with their pupils' average day. Joe's day can be done as a sketch with a pupil playing the part of Joe.

5.10 a.m. Get up and give the donkey something to eat and then start work.

11.00 a.m. Return with a cartload of rubbish to sort. Have breakfast.

11.30 a.m. Start sorting. Paper for recycling. Plastics to be cut up and remoulded. Fabric for dishcloths. Metal can be melted down. Food is given to the pig.

2.00 p.m. Lunch time for us. We have falafel (Egyptian veggie burgers) pitta bread and coffee.

2.30 p.m. My brother and sister go to school but I stay at home and help my father with the rubbish. When we have finished, I play football with my friends.

6.30 p.m. It is Thursday, so I go to church. The church is packed.

8.00 p.m. Supper.

8.30 p.m. Bedtime.

Father Samaan felt God wanted him to help his friends who worked recycling rubbish, so Father Samaan stayed and became the priest of the rubbish collectors. With his friends he started a Sunday school and helped people build proper houses, a school and a hospital.

Prayer/Reflection

Just an aluminium can recycled. One becomes many and less metal is used.

Just a jam jar recycled. One becomes many and less power is needed in factories.

Just a piece of paper recycled. One becomes many and one less tree is felled.

Thank you, Father, for all those who are involved in recycling. Help us to play our part as Father Samaan and Joe's family play theirs.

Music suggestions

'When God made the garden of Creation.' Come and Praise 1 comp. G. Marshall-Taylor (BBC 1986)

'God in his love.' Come and Praise 2, comp. G. Marshall-Taylor (BBC 1988)

'Joe's Day' adapted with permission from Tear Gas 10, a Tear Fund publication. Copyright Tear Fund 1995.
An animated video on recycling, based on Joe's family is available from Tear Fund, 100 Church Road, Teddington, Middlesex TW11 8QE.

Biblical material

Matthew 25. 31-46. Three verses are quoted below.

And God will say to those who showed love, 'When I was hungry, you fed me. When I was thirsty you gave me water to drink. When I was a stranger you welcomed me, when I was naked you clothed me, sick, you looked after me. When I was in prison, you visited me....Whatever you do to the least of my brothers, you do to me.'

You will need

A photocopy of the star of David
Paper and a thick felt-tipped pen

Introduction

Ask the pupils what things can get you into trouble at school. What might happen if people do these things? Make a list of possible consequences/punishments (handle sensitively and keep impersonal). Ask the pupils for some suggestions of ways of behaving in school for which people would normally be praised. How might people be rewarded for caring for others, sharing etc? Make a list of rewards.

Look at the two lists. Imagine punishments were given for good behaviour.

> *Sarah Grant, how dare you share your sweets! Do extra work.*

Ask the children to invent other reversed situations. This story is about a Christian who was arrested and eventually died in prison because she did all the right things.

Core material

Jane Haining was born in Scotland in 1897. She worked in Glasgow and taught in the Sunday school at her church. Jane wanted to work with children overseas and eventually became matron of a school for homeless Jewish children in Hungary. The fact that war broke out in 1939 did not stop her. She stayed in Hungary, for the school was becoming very full due to the number of Jewish children escaping from other parts of Europe. As the situation became dangerous, Jane was ordered home for her own safety but she refused to go. She felt the children needed her now more than ever.

By 1944, the Nazis had invaded Hungary and life became very hard for the children. All Jewish children had to wear a yellow star of David so that they could be identified (show pupils the yellow star). Jane helped them sew on the stars, weeping as she did so. How could people be so cruel?

In May 1944, Jane was arrested. She was accused of a number of crimes, one of them being that she had cried while sewing on the star of David. Jane was also accused of listening to the BBC, sending food parcels to prisoners, visiting prisoners, and working with Jews. Showing the kindness Jesus called for in his teaching had become a crime for which you could be punished.

Read the biblical material. Jane died in Auschwitz concentration camp for her so-called crimes. A stained glass window in Queen's Park West Church, Strathclyde, commemorates Jane's work, and each year two children from Hungary come to Scotland to visit the church which sent her. Her greatest memorial is in the lives of the children she cared for. After her death, one child wrote, 'The body of Miss Haining is dead, but she is still alive, because her smile, voice and face are still in my heart.'

Prayer/Reflection

Display the star of David. Jesus told people to help those who were sick, lonely, poor or persecuted. As we look at the star, we can remember those who suffer in war today and pray that they experience the friendship of people like Jane, whose love was matched by her courage.

Music suggestions

'Make me a channel of your peace.'
Junior Praise,
comp. P. Horrobin
and G. Leavers (Marshall Pickering 1986)

'When I needed a neighbour.' (ibid.)

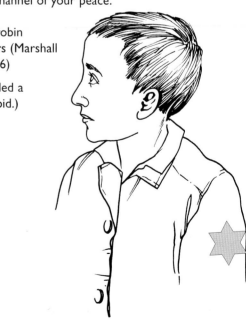

You will need

Some coloured paper squares
Some glue
Felt pen
A local newspaper with job advertisements

Introduction

Talk about duvet covers and quilts. Explain what a patchwork quilt is and ask the children to arrange the squares in a pattern as if in a quilt.

On January 25th 1992, Durham Cathedral was filled to overflowing with men and women. They met together to celebrate the work of European Christian women. During the service, a quilt made of different panels was displayed. Each panel or square represented a different Christian woman's work or life. (There were seventy two panels representing European Christian women on the quilt). This the story of just one of them: Helen Sharman, the first British astronaut.

Core material

Pupils may have seen job advertisements in a newspaper. Read out some suitable 'Wanted' advertisements. In 1989 a radio programme announced, 'Astronaut wanted - no experience necessary.' The Soviet Union was offering a place on their spacecraft to someone from Britain. A woman called Helen Sharman heard the advertisement, but she was not the only one. Thirteen thousand other people applied for the job as well!

Helen was chosen to be the first British astronaut and she spent eight days in space in May 1991.

On her section of the quilt is a space rocket (draw a rocket on one of the squares).

Before being an astronaut, Helen was a scientist working for Mars, the sweet company. After she was chosen, she went to the special training centre near Moscow in Russia. Her first job was to learn Russian, but this was no problem for Helen. She already spoke: French, German, Italian, Dutch and Japanese. Now she added Russian to her list.

Language	Hello	Pronounced
French	Bonjour	Bon-joor
German	Guten Tag	Gooten Targ
Italian	Buongiorno	Bwon-jorrno
Dutch	Hello	Hel-lo
Japanese	Koni-chua	Koh-nee-chew-ah
Russian	Priveat	Preev-ay-yat

Note: the words have been written phonetically so that pupils can enter the room and say hello in the different languages which Helen spoke.

The people at Durham Cathedral were meeting together to remember European Christian women: famous ones like Helen Sharman and those less well known. Christians come from all walks of life: they are mothers and doctors, factory workers and priests. They are even astronauts.

Prayer/ Reflection

Ask pupils to think about the range of jobs that Christian women do. These can be written up as a list. Ask pupils to look at the many and varied jobs while the prayer is read.

Thank you, Father, that you give people so many different talents and abilities. We pray that, in whatever they do, Christians will serve you and others.

Music suggestions

'In and out the stars.' Children's Praise, comp. P. Burt, P. Horrobin and G. Leavers (Marshall Pickering 1991)

'5,4,3,2,1, and Zero' and 'God who put the stars in space.' Someone's Singing Lord, B. Harrop (A and C Black 1992)

MARINO INSTITUTE OF EDUCATION

Biblical material
Matthew 6.1, 3-4

When you give something to charity, do not make a fuss about it, so that people will admire you. Give in secret, so that even your closest friend does not know. God sees what you do in private, he will reward you.

FATHER-FORGIVE

Introduction
Play a game of charades miming different jobs. Pupils can mime actions related to different jobs while the rest of the school guess what the job is. One pupil should mime 'a builder'.

Core material
On the 15th November 1940, 449 German bombers flew over the city of Coventry. Thousands of bombs were dropped: over five hundred people were killed and many more were injured. Much of the city was reduced to rubble - including the Cathedral. After the war, in 1954, a new Coventry Cathedral was designed and the Laing Company was chosen to build it. John Laing and his sons felt so privileged to be building a Cathedral that they decided to take no profit from the building work. Any money that was made was given to Cathedral funds.

John Laing was born in 1879, the son of a builder. He gradually expanded the small family firm so that it went from building houses and schools to reservoirs, aircraft hangars and finally to airstrips, major buildings and motorways.

When John first started to expand the Laing Company, he ran into trouble. He had accepted a job building sewers but the builders hit quicksand and sometimes men had to be pulled out quickly (often minus their boots). Some local people objected to the building, and the work also took twice as long as expected. Tired and depressed and facing ruin, John Laing went for a walk. He knew that the company would end if it could not pay all the bills. John was already a Christian and now he talked to God about his troubles. He made a promise to God, and wrote it down. He said that in future he would talk to God about the jobs he should do. He would not take extra money if the company did well. Instead he would give a lot of money away and put money back into the company.

John Laing was as good as his word. The company survived and grew. But John Laing did not live like a wealthy man, even though his company made millions of pounds. Instead, he gave away much of his money and put more back into the company, just as he had said he would. He was one of the first to introduce pensions and paid holidays for his workers. (You may need to explain these words.)

Although John Laing gave away much money, he did it secretly and without fuss. He remembered Jesus' words about giving. Read the biblical material.

John Laing died in 1978 aged 99. His company made millions, but when he died, he personally had only £371 in the bank.

Prayer/Reflection
Ask pupils to think for a moment about what they would do with a lot of money. For John Laing this was a reality, not a dream. He made millions. Before he was rich, he decided exactly what he would do if he ever had a lot of money and he kept his promise not to waste it or spend it selfishly.

Music suggestions
'God loves a cheerful giver' and 'The building song.' Alleluya, comp. D. Gadsby and J. Hogarth (A and C Black 1980)

Biblical material
Isaiah 59.4, 7-9

No one calls for justice, no one speaks the truth, people tell lies and act violently and no one helps the people they hurt. They have forgotten the path of peace, and justice.

You will need
A drawing of the Maltese cross (provided)
Paper and a large felt-tipped pen
Scissors
Ice cubes (optional)

Introduction
Talk about fair and unfair situations. Pupils might like to recreate some in drama. Create an 'It's not fair,' poem during the assembly lead by the teacher. Start with one line and ask the pupils to add more.

It's not fair, my brother stays up later than I do.
It's not fair.

Core material
Another word for fairness is justice. Some Christians use the Maltese Cross to remind them of justice. Show pupils the Maltese Cross. It has four arms and each arm stands for a different quality. The four qualities are: justice (fairness), perseverance (keep going), temperance (self control) and fortitude (inner strength). Today's assembly is about justice. Draw this arm of the cross very large on a sheet of paper, cut it out and write 'justice' on it (write fairness on the back so that the easier word can be shown). It is not fair or just if one person does wrong and gets away with it and another is honest and gets into trouble. Refer to the earlier examples.

Read the biblical material/write it on an acetate. This was written by Isaiah, a prophet who lived many years before Jesus was born. In his day there were many bad things going on. Ask the pupils to list some of the bad things mentioned in the reading. Isaiah saw injustice and knew that it saddened and angered God. Christians believe justice is important to God because he hates to see people he has made being hurt. Christians believe that God is just himself and he wants people to copy him.

Prayer/Reflection
Hold the arm of the cross so that it looks like an arrow pointing upwards. It looks like an arrow pointing to God, reminding people that God is just and fair and wants people to be the same.
Write up the word JUSTICE and show how it can be split into two words JUST and ICE.

Just ice

When we use the word JUST we mean 'just a little' - 'Just one minute'. It means a grudging minimum. Ice is cold, like some people's hearts. Hand out a few ice cubes, if you have them. In contrast justice is warm with feeling for others. The poem can be read by the teacher and difficult words explained.

People call for justice
But are given just -
A shrug of the shoulders,
Just words, just excuses.
People call for justice
But are given just ice.
The icy stare of the unconcerned
The icy hearts of the uncaring
Just ice instead of justice.

Music suggestions
'Whatsoever you do.' A Year of Celebration ed. J. Porter and J. McCrimmon (McCrimmons 1995)
'There is a world' (ibid.)

Biblical material

Joshua 1 (extracts)

The great leader of the Israelites, Moses, died and Joshua was chosen to be the new leader. It was a frightening moment, for he had to lead the whole nation of Israel into the Promised Land. It was also difficult to take over from someone as famous as Moses. God knew what Joshua was feeling and said this:

'Get ready, you are about to cross the Jordan River and enter your new land. Just as I was always with Moses, I will also be with you. Be strong and courageous, for you will have to lead this great nation. Be strong and very courageous. Obey the laws I gave to Moses and you will not go wrong. Be strong and courageous, don't be frightened. I will be with you wherever you go, you will not be alone.'

Joshua organised the people to cross the river and gave them their instructions.

'We will do as you say,' said the people. 'As we obeyed Moses, so we will obey you. Only be strong and courageous.'

You will need

Some small hand weights (optional)
Two paper circles (large)
Paper and scissors
A large felt-tipped pen
Sticky-Tak

Introduction

Show the weights and talk about the way some people are very strong and can lift heavy weights.

Do not ask children to lift the weights. Ask children about exercises people do to make themselves stronger. They might like to show some safe exercises such as skipping. Teachers can read some feats of physical strength taken from the Guinness Book of Records.

David Huxley single handedly pulled a Boeing 767 weighing 105 tonnes.

Cammie Lynn Lusko lifted more than her own body weight with one hand.

The Guinness Book of Records 1995, Guinness Pub Ltd (1994).

Core material

The second arm of the Maltese Cross is called fortitude. This word means strength. There are various types of strength. The Guinness Book of Records gives examples of physical strength, men and women with large muscles who can lift, pull and push great weights. There is another type of strength, inner strength. Fortitude is that inner strength. Fortitude is the ability to face difficult situations with courage. It is a strength of mind and heart. Read the biblical material. Joshua needed courage and strength for his situation: he was leader for the first time, he did not know if the people would accept him, they were about to enter a new country. What did God say to Joshua? What sort of strength did Joshua need?

Take the two circles of paper and use Blu-Tak to display them. Ask pupils to suggest times when we need inner strength. Write the situations on the circles. Cut a strip of paper to act as the bar and write 'inner strength' on it. Stick the bar between the two circles to make the shape of a weight. The bar (inner strength) allows a person to carry the weights, just as inner strength allows us to bear troubles.

Prayer/Reflection

Make the second arm of the Maltese Cross and write 'fortitude' on it. Put 'inner strength' on the other side. Display it with the previous arm so that it forms half a Maltese Cross. The extract from a hymn can be read as a prayer. Christians believe Jesus still gives them inner strength.

Fight the good fight with all your might;
Christ is your strength, and Christ your right.

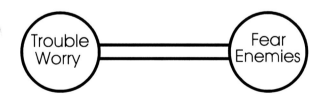

Music suggestions

'Walk with me, oh my Lord.' A Year of Celebration ed. J. Porter and J. McCrimmon (McCrimmons 1995)

'Be bold! Be strong!' Junior Praise, comp. P. Horrobin and G. Leavers (Marshall and Pickering 1986)

Biblical material

2 Peter 1.5-7

To faith add goodness,
and to goodness add knowledge,
to knowledge add temperance,
to temperance add perseverance,
to perseverance add godliness,
to godliness add brotherly kindness,
to brotherly kindness add love.

You will need

A calculator
Paper and a large felt- tipped pen
Baby walking reins

Introduction

Do some basic addition with children on the sheets of paper. Some can use the calculator. Try doing a large 'sum' where you keep adding more. Choose the numbers according to the age of your pupils. With young children add a number of objects.

7+2+6+8+2+4+6+1+9+5+10+15+5+1+0+2=?

Core material

Read the biblical material. This is like an addition sum. It keeps telling people to add more things to their lives.

Make a list of all the things the Bible says to add, the words can be simplified for younger children. Alternatively have a list of words already written which the children can put in the correct order as they listen to the reading. This assembly looks at one of these words: temperance. Temperance is an old word which means controlling yourself, not needing others to tell you what to do.

Show the baby reins and ask what they are for. When children are small they often have special reins to help them walk. They are not cruel, they stop the child wandering off and coming to harm. Very young children have to be controlled by their parents for they are not old enough to control themselves. They don't realise some things are dangerous or harmful. A young child may throw a wooden train at someone, not realising that it might hurt. To them, throwing a train is no different from throwing a teddy bear. They are too young to understand. A parent has to stop them throwing hard toys at their brothers and sisters. As we grow older, we understand what hurts others and what doesn't, and we have to learn to control ourselves in what we say and what we do. Temperance is self control - not needing other people to make us do things, but being able to control ourselves.

Prayer/Reflection

Make the third arm of the Maltese Cross as before and write 'temperance' on it and 'self control' on the other side. There should now be three arms on your cross. Older pupils can listen to the reflection below. Younger pupils can use the prayer.

The word temperance contains the smaller word 'temper'. The word temper has a double meaning. Temper means getting very angry and losing control. Temper also means 'to make strong'. Metal is tempered (worked on) to make it strong. To know how to control ourselves is to be strong, not weak.

Father, help us to control ourselves as we grow older - to control our actions and our words for the sake of those who might be hurt by them.

Music suggestions

'Sometimes I'm naughty.' Children's Praise, comp. by G. Leavers, P. Horrobin and P. Burt (Marshall Pickering 1991)

'Dear Lord and Father.' Junior Praise, comp. by P. Horrobin and G. Leavers (Marshall Pickering 1986)

Biblical material

Matthew 7.14

The gate is narrow and the path is hard that leads to life.

You will need

Paper and a large felt-tipped pen
Sticky-Tak
Scissors

Introduction

Talk with the pupils about starting things and not finishing them. If you, or pupils, have any unfinished pieces of handiwork bring them in. Ask pupils for reasons for not finishing things. Sometimes we get bored, something happens to stop us finishing them or other people put us off.

Core material

Jesus likened life to a hard path. If a path is narrow and steep it can be hard keeping to it. Make a path from paper cut like pieces of stone. Write on the 'stones' the things that make up the 'hard path' for a Christian (trust in God, truth, love, hope, caring etc). The teacher will need to give some examples.

Display the 'stones' as a pathway by fixing them along a wall.

The teacher can point to a 'stone' and ask pupils to suggest why each would be difficult. What would make someone give up and stop walking the Christian path? For example if the 'stone' is called 'truth,' people might be tempted to lie. If the 'stone' is called 'caring' people might be tempted not to bother. Short sketches can accompany the different 'stones'. Talk with the pupils about persevering (keeping going) in the face of difficulty. Jesus never said being a Christian would be easy. He said it would be like walking a hard path. Christians believe they need perseverance and help from God to walk the Christian pathway. Perseverance is that ability to keep going and not give up. It is the fourth arm of the Maltese Cross. Show the Maltese Cross and recap on the previous arms.

Prayer/Reflection

Make the fourth arm of the Maltese cross as before. Write 'perseverance' on one side and 'keeping going' on the other side. Hold it up like an arrow while the prayer is said. Either read the poem or say the prayer. The poem 'Uphill' by Christina Rossetti communicates the feeling of the Christian journey being a hard one.

Uphill
Does the road wind uphill all the way?
Yes, to the very end.
Will the day's journey take the whole long day?
From morn to night, my friend.

Father, help us to persevere in the face of difficulty. It is easy to start and give up once life becomes hard.

Music suggestions

'The journey of life.' Come and Praise 1, comp. G. Marshall-Taylor (BBC 1986)

'He who would valiant be.' (ibid.)

You will need

A plastic bucket
A driving licence

Introduction

Ask pupils if they know the song, 'There's a hole in my bucket'? If pupils know this they might like to sing it or the words can be read. Point out that the bucket in question would probably be a metal one: what are most of our buckets made of today? Nowadays, if our bucket had a hole in it, we would probably throw it away and buy a new one. Once buckets, saucepans and kettles were so expensive that people would repair them as many times as possible. Men called 'tinkers' used to travel round the villages and towns shouting something like, 'Kettles! Saucepans! Get them mended here!' This was their job - to repair people's cooking pots. One of these tinkers was called John Bunyan.

Core material

John Bunyan was born in a village near Bedford in 1628. His family was not rich, and he did not spend long at school: but he did learn to read and write. He lived through a dangerous and difficult time in Britain: the Civil War (1642-1649). (Explain that a civil war is when two groups inside a country fight each other.) Even friends and families found themselves fighting each other as the King (Charles I) and Parliament fought to control the country. Bunyan himself fought on the side of Parliament. The king was captured and executed, and Parliament ruled for several years. Then the dead king's son (Charles II) was crowned king. Christians, called Puritans, who had sided with Parliament during the war, were unpopular with the new king. (Just explain that there was a war going on to younger pupils.)

John Bunyan was a tinker, but he had another job, too, an unpaid job. He spent all his spare time and every Sunday travelling round the villages to tell people about God (preaching). In those days you needed a licence to preach, just as you need a licence to drive now (show the licence). Driving without a licence is against the law. In those days, preaching without a licence was against the law, and the authorities often refused to give Puritans, such as John Bunyan, a licence. He carried on preaching, even though he knew it might get him into trouble. In the end, he was arrested while he was preaching in a field, and thrown into prison. For the next 12 years, John spent most of his time in prison, because he refused to stop preaching what he believed was the truth about God. In the years he spent in prison, John found another way to tell people about God: he began to write books. And one of those books is still famous today. It is called *The Pilgrim's Progress*.

Prayer/Reflection

Enlarge and display the illustration. Ask some pupils to Blu-Tak some paper 'bars' over him. Read and explain Bunyan's verse.

He that is down need fear no fall
He that is low, no pride.
He that is humble ever shall
Have God to be his guide.

Music suggestions

'One more step along the road I go' or 'Travel on.' The Complete Come and Praise, comp. G. Marshall-Taylor (BBC 1990)

Note: Over these ten assemblies, a display of Christian's journey can be created. A strip of paper is added to the display on most days to represent the path along which Christian travelled. Have eight strips already cut. You should also have paper, scissors, felt tips and Blu-Tak ready for each assembly besides the items mentioned in the 'You will need' section.

You will need

Two sets of cards, one with the italicised words from the hymn below, one with their definitions

Introduction

Talk with pupils about journeys they have been on. What sort of difficulties might someone meet on a journey? What good things might happen? Write up some of their suggestions.

Core material

John Bunyan was in prison because he would not stop telling people about God. While he was there he realised that he could write about God. He wrote a book about a made up person called Christian. The book was called *The Pilgrim's Progress*. A pilgrim is someone who goes on a journey for religious reasons - to visit somewhere special or to keep a promise they have made to God. This book tells about the journey Christian makes to get to heaven. We are told how he 'progresses' or 'gets on' with this journey. The people and events in this book stand for, or are pictures of, other things. Christian is a picture of any person who decides to follow God. His journey is a picture of the difficulties and pleasures that anybody might meet as they try to follow God.

The hymn below is based on Bunyan's writings. It tells us about the sort of journey Christian had and about the problems he faced. Infants can listen to the tape of the song (Come Praise 1 Cassette BBC ISBN 374780). Explain that this is a song Bunyan wrote about not giving up even when things are difficult or dangerous.

> 'He who would *valiant* be
> 'Gainst all disaster,
> Let him in *constancy*
> Follow the *Master*.
> There's no *discouragement*
> Shall make him once *relent*
> His first *avowed intent*
> To be a *pilgrim*.'

Some of these words need an explanation. Give out the cards of the italicised words. Then give out the definition set at random. Ask the pupils to match word and meaning. (valiant = brave; constancy = faithfulness, perseverance; Master = Jesus; discouragement = feeling you want to give up; relent = give up; avowed intent = the promise he has given; pilgrim = someone who goes on a journey for religious reasons.)

When the words have been correctly matched, read the verses again: do the pupils think that this journey is going to be easy or hard? Ask for reasons for their answer.

Younger pupils. The first two assemblies can be combined into one. Use the introduction to Bunyan as a tinker, and then go on to this assembly, explaining that he was in prison because he would not stop telling people about Jesus. So he found another way of telling them. The explanation of the book's title can be used. Excerpts from the hymn can be read out and the pupils questioned as to what sort of journey this is going to be.

Prayer/Reflection

Display the words of the song and the cards. Listen to the tape or read the prayer.

Father, as we travel through life, give us courage to face difficult times, rest when we are tired, and love to share with others on the journey.

Music suggestions

'He who would valiant be.' The Complete Come and Praise, comp. G. Marshall-Taylor (BBC 1990)

This can be learnt a verse at a time over several days. For younger children: 'One more step along the road I go' or 'Travel on' from the same source.

Giant Despair

You will need
Name cards - Christian; City of Destruction; Teller of Good News
Enough Lego for two teams of two children to make recognisable houses

Introduction
Before you start, set two teams, of two children each, to make houses out of the Lego. The names of the people in the book *The Pilgrim's Progress* are very important: they have a meaning that will tell us about them. Many of our last names used to be like this. Once, people called Smith really were smiths - blacksmiths, who made things out of iron. Here are some other names that used to tell other people what their owners did: Baker and Farmer.

Core material
(During this part of the assembly, ask three pupils to hold up the name cards in turn). In the part of the story we are hearing today, there is a man called Christian: his name tells us that he believed in Jesus Christ. He lived in a place called the City of Destruction. Ask the two teams to show their houses. Then deliberately destroy them. (Warn them you are going to do this beforehand.) Ask them what they felt about your behaviour. Tell the pupils that this is what life in the City of Destruction was like - full of cruelty and unhappiness. Do they think that Christian was happy living in this city? But one day, he heard someone talking about God - and this man was called Teller of Good News, (or Evangelist). The good news he was telling was that God wanted Christian to leave the city and go to live with him. How do they think this made Christian feel? He decided to leave straightaway, and here is the beginning of his journey.

The story: Christian leaves the City of Destruction
Christian lived in the City of Destruction. At first he was happy, but then he became sure that the way he lived did not please God. He was greatly upset, because he did not know how to become God's friend. He also knew he had done many things wrong and this troubled him and it was like a great load on his back. One day he met a man called Teller of Good News (or Evangelist) who told him that the way to be friends with God and to live with him forever in heaven was to go through a small, narrow door or gate in a wall. (This door was called the Wicket Gate.) So Christian set off for the Gate.

Younger pupils. It is sometimes easier, with the rest of these assemblies, to use the story as the framework for the whole assembly, introducing the other elements as you go. A suggested plan for each one is given. Use the house-building activity, then tell the story, pausing to introduce the names and their meanings as you come to them.

Prayer/Reflection
Enlarge and display the illustrations and add Christian (page 91) and the Gate (page 40). Add the first strip to the path and the name cards.

Sometimes a journey seems very long and it is difficult to start. But however long a journey is, each one starts with one step. Christian started his journey by turning his back on the City of Destruction and walking towards friendship with God.

Music suggestions (See page 38)

You will need

Large circles of paper. Cut the centre out of each circle and label the inner circles as follows: 'I will never leave you', 'I will never reject you', 'I will always love you'.
Other pieces of paper, cut in 'puddle' shapes
Name cards: Help and the Swamp of Sadness

Introduction

Make sure everyone knows what stepping stones are, and what the result would be of falling off them. Lay the paper rings on the floor. Fix them with a little Blu-Tak so that they do not slip. Explain that they are stepping-stones over a very sticky, smelly swamp (discuss what this is). Ask for a volunteer to walk over them, looking at them as they cross. Was it easy to stay on the stepping-stones? Now ask another pupil to walk over them while keeping their gaze fixed on a point on the far wall. Was this more difficult? Recap on the story so far. In the story today, Christian has to get over a swamp. Hold up the name cards and explain their meaning.

The Gate

The story: Christian gets stuck!

Now as Christian walked towards the Wicket Gate, he stumbled into a sticky swamp called the Swamp of Sadness (or Slough of Despond). It was the place where all the travellers' fears and doubts gathered together and tried to stop them going on. Christian struggled on even though he felt like giving up. Then a man appeared called Help, and he helped Christian out of the sticky mud. 'Why didn't you remember God's promises?' he asked him. 'They would have helped you through this swamp, because they are so firm and strong that they would have been like stepping stones for you.'

Core material

The Swamp of Sadness was made up of all the things that could have stopped Christian from going on with his journey. What do they think these things were? Draw out such things as people making fun of him; loneliness; unhappiness. Write some of the suggestions on the 'puddle' shapes. Spread these around the stepping stones to represent the swamp or marsh. When Help found him there, he told him that God's promises were like stepping stones to help people across all these unpleasant things. Place the promise circles inside the rings and fix them with Blu-Tak. Show the pupils how the promises have become firm ground on which the traveller can stand. Ask a pupil to cross on them slowly, reading out each promise as they step on it. Do they remember that it was easier to cross when the person looked at the stones? This is a picture of what Christian was meant to do. If he had kept his eyes and his mind on God's promises, he would have been safe. It would have been easy to stay on the path. Christians believe that God keeps his promises. They try to remember these promises when they are worried or in trouble. Then their worries and troubles do not defeat them.

Younger pupils. Start with the story, but have the rings of the stepping stones already in place. Describe them when you arrive at the swamp. Explain what the swamp is and lay down the named 'puddles'. Demonstrate walking on the stones yourself, and begin to 'sink'. Continue with Help, and his explanation. Add the promises to the stones, and use the paragraph about Christian trusting in God's promises.

Help

Prayer/Reflection

Blu-Tak some puddles and stepping stones to the wall. Enlarge and display Help and the Swamp of Sadness (page 91). Add another strip to the path and the name cards. Ask pupils to think about people who have helped them on their journey through life.

Music suggestions
(See page 38)

You will need
A rucksack and a label reading 'Guilt'
Requirements for a few days' hiking (e.g. sleeping bag, cooking utensils, food, clothes, etc.)
Name card: The Man who Explained
Some weights (500g, 1 kg etc.)

Introduction
Explain that you going hiking for several days. Ask the children what you will have to take beside a tent. Pack them as they suggest them, or ask some pupils to pack them. Talk about how heavy the rucksack is, and how difficult it will be to carry it for several days. There are a lot of things that you have to take, heavy though they are. Ask two pupils to unpack the rucksack quietly while you continue talking. Recap on the story so far.

Core material
Christian continued his journey but it was not easy because he was carrying a very heavy load. But his rucksack did not hold things he needed. Instead, it held things he wanted to get rid of! The load he carried was called 'Guilt'. Label the rucksack. Explain the meaning of guilt, and discuss how feeling guilty about something makes us feel miserable. Christian knew that he had done many things wrong, and he felt guilty about them. He felt so guilty that it was like carrying a heavy load on his back - and he couldn't get rid of it no matter what he did. Write some 'wrongs' (stealing, lying etc.) on pieces of paper. Ask pupils to wrap each weight in one piece of paper with a 'wrong' written on it and place it in the rucksack. Do not ask pupils to carry the rucksack but explain how heavy it is. Introduce The Man who Explained who appears in today's story. (Hold up the name card.)

The story: Christian loses his load
Christian went through the Gate in the wall, and now he was on the road to friendship with God. He stayed for a while at the House of the Man who Explained (or the Interpreter). This man explained many things to him about his journey and about what it meant to be a follower of God. He told him how important it was to stay on the path at all times. Then Christian

travelled on. There ahead of him, on a hill, he saw the cross. He ran to it, and as he looked at it, the great load of wrong things he had done fell off his back, and rolled down the hill and into a grave dug there. And Christian never saw those things again, and he never again had to carry them. He was given new clothes to wear, and a scroll of paper with his name and God's word on it. He was reminded again to stay on the path whatever happened. Then he continued on his journey.

Younger pupils. Begin - 'Christian continued his journey,' but do not introduce the man who Explained. Tell the story omitting, The Man who Explained, just saying that Christian was told he must stay on the path.

Prayer/Reflection
Display the rucksack. Ask pupils to look at it while you read the reflection. Enlarge and display the illustrations. Add a strip to the path and the name card *or* the instruction to stay on the path.

Christian felt weighed down by wrong and guilt. It was like carrying a heavy rucksack. The message of Jesus was that people do not have to carry this weight: there is forgiveness.

Music suggestions
'The journey of life.' The Complete Come and Praise, comp. G. Marshall-Taylor (BBC 1990)

You will need
Name cards: Hill of Difficulty; Danger; Destruction; Palace Beautiful; Peace; Enjoyable Mountains

Introduction
Ask pupils to think for a moment about their favourite place - the place they would most like to be. We all have favourite places - and we also have places we do not like! Recap on the story so far and ask pupils what Christian was told he must do (stay on the path).

Core material
The story today has several places, some of which were pleasant places to be, and others that were horrible. The first one is called the Hill of Difficulty. (Hold up the name card.) Discuss the meaning of difficult.

What do you think this hill was like? Would it be easy for Christian to climb over this hill? There were two paths round the hill so that travellers did not have to climb it. They were called Danger and Destruction. (Hold up the name cards.) What would these other ways or paths be like? Would they be worse than the hill or easier?

Then Christian arrived at a house called the Palace Beautiful. (Hold up the name.) Hold up an enlarged copy of the palace. What would the pupils expect to find in this? Point out that it is not just material things that make a building beautiful to us. That night, Christian went to sleep in a room called Peace. What would this room be like? Ask the pupils to close their eyes and to think for a few moments about a room called Peace. In the morning, Christian was told that his path would eventually lead him to the Enjoyable Mountains. (Show the name card.) These mountains were so beautiful that people enjoyed just being there. However, the mountains were in the distance and he had to face more trouble before he reached them.

The story: The Hill of Difficulty
Two other pilgrims joined Christian, and soon they came to a steep hill. Now the path they had been told to follow led right over this hill, and this hill was called Difficulty. Christian's two friends said, 'It would be far too difficult to climb

that hill! We are going round it!' And they did: one went one way, and the other went the other way. And neither of them were seen again, for the ways round the hill were called Danger and Destruction. But Christian struggled up the hill. He knew that he must stay on the path, even if it was hard to do so. The Interpreter had warned him that the way was not easy. And, at last, he reached a great house that was called the Palace Beautiful. God had set this house there for pilgrims to rest in, and Christian slept well in a bedroom called Peace. There, he was given armour for the journey and he was shown the Enjoyable (or Delectable) Mountains in the distance. 'That is where the path lies,' the people told him, and he set off once more.

Younger pupils. Tell the story, explaining and using the names and the Palace (and the text relating to them) as you reach them.

Prayer/Reflection
Enlarge and display the illustrations. Add a strip to the path and add the name cards.

Often we have to face difficulties in order to do what is right, just as Christian had to climb the Hill of Difficulty in order to get to the Palace Beautiful and the Enjoyable Mountains.

Music suggestions
'Father, I place into Your hands' or 'When the road is rough and steep.' Junior Praise 1, comp. P. Horrobin and G. Leavers (Marshall Pickering 1986)

You will need
Name cards: Apollyon; Valley of Fear; Faithful

Introduction
Recap on the story so far and ask them what Christian was told he must do (stay on the path). Ask a pupil to hold up the Faithful card. Christian meets a man called Faithful - but what does this mean? Discuss with the pupils the idea of faithfulness in friends.

Core material
There is a place in the story called The Valley of Fear (hold up the name card). Here, Christian seemed to meet all the things he had ever been frightened of. And in the valley was a monster! He was like all of Christian's fears rolled up in one horrible body! He was called Apollyon (hold up his name card.) Can you imagine what this 'Fear Monster' looked like? Bunyan said that it was made up of all the frightening animals he could think of. Let's design our own 'Fear Monster'. Take suggestions for its body, head, eyes, feet, skin, etc., and draw it on the sheet.

Let's see how Christian escapes from the Valley of Fear. You can decide if our monster or Bunyan's is more frightening!

The story: The Valley of Fear
Christian soon needed his armour! In the valley below the hill, he met a monster called Apollyon! Now this monster had wings like a dragon, feet like a bear, a mouth like a lion, out of which came fire and smoke, and he was covered with scales like a fish! When Apollyon heard where Christian had come from and where he was going, he tried to make him return home. 'If you return now, I will be kind to you. You are

not good enough to be God's friend, anyway!' But Christian refused to give up, and so the monster attacked him. It was a long and hard fight, and Christian was almost defeated. But he fought on, and at last he wounded Apollyon with his sword and drove him away. But even worse was to come, for the valley was the Valley of Fear where death is close to the travellers (or the Valley of the Shadow of Death). And here Christian almost gave up. His sword was no help here against his terror. Instead, he prayed to God, asking him to be with him. And he heard, in the distance ahead of him, someone saying, 'Even though I am in this valley, I will not be afraid, because you, God, are here with me.' Then Christian knew that he was not alone. Someone else was in the valley. At the end of the Valley he met the other pilgrim, and his name was Faithful, and they became good friends.

Younger pupils. Tell the story, acting it out as you speak if you can. When the monster appears, break off and create the 'Fear Monster' or ask pupils to do this. (Emphasise the imaginary nature of these monsters and the defeat of Christian's monster). We all have different ideas of what is frightening. Read them Bunyan's description of his 'Fear Monster'. Tell about the fight, and the Valley of Fear and Faithful. Ask what sort of person Faithful is.

Prayer/Reflection
Enlarge and display the illustrations. Add a strip to the path, add the name cards. Read the extract from Psalm 23.

Even though I go through the Valley of the Shadow of Death I will fear no evil, for you are with me.

Music suggestions
'The Lord's my shepherd' or 'When I am feeling lonely.' Children's Praise, comp. P. Burt, P. Horrobin and G. Leavers (Marshall Pickering 1991)

You will need
Name cards: Lord Hategood; Mr. No-good; Mr. Liar; Mr. Cruelty; Hopeful; Good Will; Patience; Faithful; Emptiness

Introduction
Recap on the story so far and ask the pupils what Christian has to remember to do (stay on the path). In the last assembly, we thought about some of the places with special names. Today, we are going to meet a lot of people who had special names.

Core material
The travellers have arrived in a town called Emptiness or Vanity Fair. (Hold up the name card.) Bunyan called it this because nothing in that town was really worth anything (vanity here means emptiness). Christian's friend, Faithful, told the people this, and they were so angry that they arrested him and put him on trial. The Judge was called Lord Hategood (give each name card to a pupil as you mention it), and some of the people who had to decide if Faithful was guilty or not were called Mr. No-good, Mr. Liar, and Mr. Cruelty. How would these people behave? Discuss each in turn: would Faithful get a fair trial from them?

There are many other names in this book that we have not yet met. Read out Hopeful, Goodwill, Patience and Faithful and hand out their name cards. Explain their meanings as necessary. Christian would have been pleased to meet some of these people, and horrified to meet others. Ask for a pair of volunteers to sort the names into these two groups. Comment on their results.

The Town of Emptiness

The story: Vanity Fair or the Town of Emptiness
As Faithful and Christian travelled on they came to a town called Emptiness (or Vanity Fair). The people who lived here tried to stop all the pilgrims going any further. 'All you want is here!' they told them. 'Don't risk your lives going on. Stay here and enjoy yourselves for the rest of your lives!' Faithful and Christian said that none of the things in the town was important. 'All that matters is to follow God!' they told them. Then the people were angry, and they put them on trial. The judge's name was Lord Hategood, and some of the men on the jury were called Mr. No-good, Mr. Liar, and Mr. Cruelty. They decided to kill Faithful because he refused to stop following God. They let Christian go. And a man called Hopeful, who had secretly agreed with Faithful, went with Christian as a pilgrim.

Lord Hategood & Friends

Younger pupils. Introduce the idea of names that reflect character by using the *Mr. Men* or *Little Miss* books. Tell the story, introducing the names and the text about them when you reach Faithful's trial. Continue with the story.

Prayer/Reflection
Enlarge and display the illustrations. Add a strip to the path. Ask pupils to imagine that John Bunyan was writing about them. What name would they like him to give them?

Music suggestions
'A still small voice' or 'Father, hear the prayer we offer.' The Complete Come and Praise, comp. G. Marshall-Taylor (BBC 1990)

You will need
Name cards: Giant Despair; Doubting Castle; Promise
A photocopy of the key
Strips of sugar paper to form prison 'bars': one side of each strip blank, the others each with one of these words on:- despair, unhappiness, loneliness, giving up

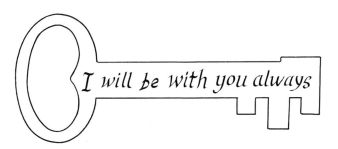

I will be with you always

Introduction
Recap on the story so far and ask the pupils what Christian has to remember to do (stay on the path). In today's story, Christian and Hopeful find themselves in a prison - but it is not an ordinary prison! It is the dungeon of a castle called Doubting Castle (Show the name card).

Core material
Talk about the meaning of 'doubt'. Explain that Christian had begun to doubt that he could trust the promises of God. God had promised that he would reach the Heavenly (or Celestial) City and he had promised that he would keep him safe on the way. Now, Christian thinks that he will never reach the City, and that God will not help him because Christian had done the one thing he was told not to do: he had left the path to find an easier way. The owner of this castle, who throws them into the dungeon, is called Giant Despair. Explain the meaning of despair and show the name card. The giant tries to make them give up hope, telling them that they are no good at all and that God does not want them. Let's find out if they escape.

The story: Giant Despair
Now, Christian began to think that he knew all he needed to know about this journey. When they came to a place where the path was very rough and difficult, he told Hopeful, 'Look! There is another, easier path that runs next to our path. Let's take that one instead!' So Christian left the proper path, and took Hopeful with him. They soon realised they were

wrong, but as they walked back to the correct path, they were captured by Giant Despair, and put into dungeons at his home, Doubting Castle. Giant Despair did all he could to make them give up their journey. He gave them no food, and he whipped them. He threatened to kill them and he reminded them of all the times they had failed to obey God. At last, though, Christian remembered that he had been given a special key and this key was called Promise (Show the key). It would open any door anywhere. So the two pilgrims crept out of the castle and continued their journey.

Younger pupils. Tell the story, pausing to introduce Giant Despair and Doubting Castle as you reach them.

Prayer/Reflection
Write the suggested words on long strips of paper, and have these held up in front of two pupils playing Christian and Hopeful in prison. When they remember the key, these 'bars' of the door can be dropped to show their freedom. Show the pupils the key. Read out the promise on it, the promise was like a key to the prisoners, releasing them from their despair and worry which had become like a prison.

Enlarge and display the illustrations and Giant Despair (page 38). Add a strip to the path and the name cards.

Music suggestions
'My faith it is an oaken staff' or 'When the road is rough and steep' Junior Praise 1, comp. P. Horrobin and G. Leavers (Marshall Pickering 1986)

Doubting Castle

You will need
Name cards: Heavenly City; Enjoyable Mountains (already used)

Introduction
Recap on the story so far and ask the pupils what Christian has to remember to do (stay on the path).

Core material
All Christian wanted was to get to the Heavenly City (Show the name card). He started off from a very different city: ask pupils if they remember what it was called. What do they think the City of Destruction looked like? The Heavenly City looked very different! Bunyan says that it was made of gold - its roads and its buildings! And its buildings were covered in pearls and precious stones. Life in the Heavenly City was peaceful, and the people living in it were so precious to God that they were surrounded with precious and beautiful things. But the cities did not just look different. Life inside them was very different, too. Recap on life in the City of Destruction. The Bible says this about life in the Heavenly City or Heaven: 'God will wipe away every tear. No one will die, no one will be unhappy. There will be no crying and there will be no pain. Everything will be new.' Christians believe that the best thing about Heaven is that God will live there with his friends.

The story: The Heavenly City
And now at last they reached the Enjoyable (or Delectable) Mountains. There, they rested for a while and then they travelled on. It wasn't long before they came to a place from where they could see the Heavenly City. 'At last!' Christian said. 'Soon we will be with God, and nothing will ever frighten or hurt us again.' But in between them and the City flowed a great river! (Show the name card). 'I cannot swim across this!' Christian said, and he was very unhappy. Surely God was not going to leave him alone and without help after the long journey.

Other people told him, 'This is the only way into the city!' So he and Hopeful plunged in and began to swim. But soon Christian grew tired. It seemed to him that he could not reach the other shore, and he began to sink.

Hopeful shouted to him, 'Remember what we have been told. Jesus will look after us!'

Then Christian heard Jesus' voice, and it was saying, 'When you cross the river, I will be with you. I will not let the waters drown you.' And he realised that he was safe, and swam on. And very soon, they came to the shore, and entered the Heavenly City, where God lives. God welcomed them into his home with great joy. And their journey was over at last.

Younger pupils. Tell the story, introducing the places as you reach them.

Prayer/Reflection
Add the last piece of path and the name cards. Enlarge and display the illustrations.

Life is like a journey. Christian's journey was over but his new life with God was only just beginning.

Music suggestions
'He who would valiant be' or 'The journey of life.' The Complete Come and Praise, comp. G. Marshall-Taylor (BBC 1990)

Biblical material

I Samuel 19.9-18

You will need

A pillow and blanket
Something furry for hair

Introduction

Ask pupils to imagine someone wanted to pretend they were in bed when really they were not. Show them how it could be done with a pillow and some fur, or ask pupils to demonstrate. Place the pillow on a table, cover it with a blanket and place the fur in the right position for hair. This is not advice on how to trick your parents! It is what happens in one story from the Bible.

Core material

Michal loved her husband David. But this evening, as she waited for David to return from the palace, she was very worried. For her father, King Saul, was trying to kill David! She had suspected this for a long time. She had heard stories about Saul throwing his spear at David twice. Then David had been sent out to lead his men against the Philistines over and over again, because Saul hoped that he would be killed in battle. Saul had even told David that he could not marry Michal until he had killed one hundred Philistines! 'My father is so jealous,' she thought as she paced to and fro. 'He knows the people love David more than they love him.' Then, at last, she heard David: he was home. But he was upset. 'He's tried to kill me again!' he told her. Michal was heart-broken. Lying awake that night, she heard footsteps out in the street. She crept to the window and looked out. Saul's soldiers - waiting for David!

'You must leave now!' she told him. 'They're waiting outside ready to kill you in the morning.' David hurriedly got ready. They went to a back room, and Michal helped him to escape through a window. Then she started work. She found a statue about David's size and rolled it over to the bed. She covered it with the blanket, and then found some goat hair from the loom, and laid it around the statue's head - that would look like David's hair! Then she waited.

In the morning, Saul's soldiers burst in to take David by surprise. Michal stopped them at the bedroom door. 'He's ill,' she told them. 'He can't come with you.'

Saul was furious when he heard this. 'Bring him to me on his bed then!' he roared. 'I can kill him just as well lying down as standing up!' The soldiers rushed back.

Pushing Michal aside, they ran over to the bed - and found the statue! Then they knew they were in trouble. They took Michal to Saul to explain what she had done. 'You have tricked me - your father- and let my enemy escape!' he shouted.

Michal told him the story she had made up ready. 'He made me do it!' she said. But all the time she was thinking, 'He's safe now! He's had plenty of time to reach friends. I've done it!'

Michal tricked her father, King Saul, because she wanted to save her husband David's life. David was young, handsome, talented and brave. Saul was jealous. In the end, the only thing Michal could do was to play a trick on her father in order to let David escape to safety. There were no good options for Michal, she either had to deceive her father or let her husband be captured: she chose the best in the situation. The situation did not make the trick right, it was the 'least bad' thing she could do.

Prayer/Reflection

Ask pupils to think about times when they have had to make difficult decisions. The prayer below can be read.

There are times, Father, when we have difficult decisions to make, when no course of action seems right. Guide our thoughts and our actions in those moments to do the best possible in the situation.

Music suggestions

'Sometimes problems can be BIG.' Children's Praise, comp. P. Burt, P. Horrobin and G. Leavers (Marshall Pickering 1991)

'Father, I place into your hands.' Junior Praise 1, comp. P. Horrobin and G. Leavers (Marshall Pickering 1986)

Biblical material
Luke 2.29-32

Lord, you have done what you
promised,
Now I feel I can go in peace.
With my own eyes I have seen your
rescuer,
The one you have sent for all people.
He will be like a light for all the
nations
and for his people Israel.

You will need
A timer that will 'ping'
A gift wrapped parcel

Introduction
Ask for complete silence and set the timer for one
minute. Tell the pupils you have received a present
from your Aunt Peggy, but in her letter she said you
could not open it until ....(add the time that suits
your assembly). Ask them to wait for one minute, tell
them the 'pinger' will sound when one minute is over,
and that then you can open your present. Place the
parcel in a prominent position and look longingly at it
while you wait. You will need to put something in the
parcel that children will enjoy seeing you unwrap.
When the time is up, unwrap the present and ask
pupils how easy or difficult it was to wait. Share your
own feelings about waiting.

Core material
In the Bible, there is a story about two people who
had to wait many years for a present. Their names
were Simeon and Anna. Many years before, they had
each been told by God that they would one day meet
God's special king or rescuer. For years they had
waited, and now they were very old. Simeon and Anna
spent every day in the Temple praying, hoping that
each day would be the day they would meet the
special king.

One day, Simeon saw a young couple come into the
temple. They were poor and were carrying a small
baby. Simeon knew this was the one. He took the baby
in his arms and told Mary and Joseph of the great
things their child, Jesus, would do, but warned them
that his life would be hard.

Simeon's poem can be still be found in the Bible (read
the biblical material). Later, Anna saw the couple. She,
too, knew that this child was special and pointed him
out to others in the Temple. All this happened just
after Jesus' birth. For Anna and Simeon it was like a
late Christmas present, for which they had waited a
long time. Today, some Christians celebrate this story
in a service called Candlemas, held on February 2nd. In
this service candles are blessed and lit candles are
often carried in procession. For Christians, it is a
reminder of the words of Simeon, that Jesus came as
'light' for all the world.

Prayer/Reflection
Ask pupils to think quietly of something for which
they waited a long time but considered that it was
worth waiting for. If appropriate, light a candle and
repeat the phrase 'The Light of the World' in different
languages.

La Luce de Mondo (Italian)
Das Licht der Welt (German)
Lumière du Monde (French)

Music suggestions
'Light of all the World.' Rejoice 1, comp. A. White
(Harper Collins Religious 1993)

'If I were a star.' Feeling Good, P. Churchill (The
National Society/Church House Publishing 1994)

Biblical material
Luke 1.5-24, 57-66 See the story below.

You will need
A baby name book

Introduction
Talk with the pupils about baby names. Ask them what name they would choose for a boy or a girl.

Explain that in this story the parents were told what to call their child: he was to be called John. John is a name we still use today. It means 'God is gracious' (loving).

Core material
Elizabeth and Zechariah were John's parents. Elizabeth was old. All her life she had wanted children but as the years went by she lost hope. Now she was holding her baby son in her arms. All the neighbours and relatives had come to celebrate. Somehow they had crammed into the tiny house. The baby was a week old, so it was time to give him his name.

Elizabeth thought back to the events of nearly a year ago. It had all started in the Temple at Jerusalem. Her husband, Zechariah, was a priest. He had been on duty at the Temple taking part in the daily service. He was burning sweet smelling incense on the altar when an angel appeared. Zechariah was alarmed.

'Don't be afraid,' said the angel. 'Your prayers have been answered.'

'Which prayers?' thought Zechariah to himself. 'I have prayed many!'

'You and Elizabeth shall have a son and he shall be called John. He will make you and many others happy by his birth. He will be a great man like the prophets of old. He will get people ready for God's special king who will come soon.'

'I am old,' said Zechariah. 'So is Elizabeth, my wife. How do I know this is true?'

'I am Gabriel,' replied the angel, 'the messenger of God. You will be unable to speak until the baby is born as you have not believed this good news.'

Elizabeth remembered the shock of seeing her husband being unable to speak, but he had written down what had happened, explaining what the angel had said. Soon Elizabeth and Zechariah realised it was all true, for Elizabeth was expecting Zechariah's child.

That had been many months ago. Now the baby was safely born and needed a name. The neighbours crowded round. 'What are you going to call him?' asked one. 'He ought to be called Zechariah after his father.'

'No,' said Elizabeth. 'His name is John!'

'John?' questioned a relative. 'None of your family are called John.'

Everyone looked at Zechariah and made signs asking him what the baby should be called. Zechariah signed for something to write with, and wrote these words. 'His name is John.'

At that moment Zechariah regained his speech and the angel's words came true. John's birth brought much joy and happiness.

Prayer/Reflection
John and Jesus, two children whose births brought joy, not only to their parents but also to others: as we approach Christmas, may we remember the birth of John, the one who prepared people for Jesus, as well as the birth of Jesus himself.

Music suggestions
'A voice cries out .' A Year of Celebration, ed. by J. Porter and J. McCrimmon (McCrimmons 1995)

'Advent wreath song.' (ibid.)

Biblical material
See page 89 (Manna)

You will need
A large felt tipped pen
Paper or overhead transparency
Blu-Tak

Introduction
Talk about the different titles people can have and what they tell you about them.

Sir

Duke   King

Lady   **Duchess**

PRESIDENT   *Queen*

Core material
Throughout the Bible, God is given various titles. These titles tell people something about him. Copy and display the various titles of God and ask pupils what they might tell Christians about him.

Example: He is called 'the Shield', for Christians believe he is a protector in the ups and down of life, like a shield in battle. He is called 'Almighty' to show he is powerful or mighty. He is called 'the Rock' because people can depend on him. He is called 'Most High' because Christians think he is more important than anyone else.

God 'Almighty'   *God 'Most High'*

God 'the Shield'   God 'the Rock'

When the Israelites were wandering in the wilderness, after they had escaped as slaves from Egypt, they needed food. God gave them food in the ordinary way - through animals and things that grew - as they went on the journey. The Bible says God also gave them food in a different way. Read the story of the manna in the desert.

God provided for the Israelites all through their journey so the Israelites gave him the name 'God the Provider or Giver'. Christians believe God still provides or gives food. Every Harvest, they celebrate God giving through the food that grows in the world he created. They believe he made the world so that it would provide food for humanity, for our world produces more than enough food to feed everyone.

Prayer/Reflection
Use the following prayer as an example of a Christian expression of thanks.
'All good gifts around us are sent from Heaven above.
Then thank the Lord, O thank the Lord
For all his love.'

(M.Claudius 1740-1815. Translated by Jane Campbell 1817-1878)

Music suggestions
'Share it round.' Feeling Good, P. Churchill (The National Society/Church House Publishing 1994)

'Now we sing a harvest song.' The Complete Come and Praise, comp. G. Marshall-Taylor (BBC 1990)

Biblical material

See the parable of the prodigal son on page 87.

You will need

Eleven pieces of card
A cardboard medal with a ribbon
A cushion on which to rest the medal
A large sheet of paper and a pen

Introduction

Hold up the medal and say that you would like to award it to someone who is:

reliable	listens to your point of view
has time for you	lets you have your own way sometimes
doesn't treat you badly	trusts you
is kind but not soft	doesn't embarrass you
is fair	loves you
remembers you need things (like pocket money)	

Have each of the qualities above written on the pieces of card and ask eleven pupils to come and hold up the cards. On the back of each card have one letter of the word superparent so that the cards spell that word when turned over. Look round for someone to whom you could award the medal. Explain that you are looking for a superparent, someone with all these qualities. Ask the pupils to turn over their cards and spell superparent.

Core material

Explain that not everyone lives with their mum and dad. Some people have one parent, some have a parent who has died, others have foster parents, but most of us have an idea of an ideal parent. No parent, however good, lives up to the ideal of a superparent.

Christians believe God is like an ideal parent. Jesus told the story of the prodigal son to help people understand that God is like a father, not just any father, but an ideal one: a superparent. Read the story on page 87. After reading the story, draw out parallels between the father in the story of the prodigal son and the qualities on the cards.

Prayer/Reflection

Ask pupils to hold up the cards again, one at a time. Pupils should look up, think about one or two qualities, then spend a few seconds thinking about them in relation to the story of the prodigal son.

Music suggestions

'God knows my name.' Children's Praise, comp. G. Leavers and P. Burt (Marshall Pickering 1991)

'Father, I place into your hands.' Junior Praise, comp. P. Horrobin and G. Leavers (Marshall Pickering 1986)

Biblical material
Psalm 90.2

Before the mountains were created, you were there, God. Before the earth was made, you existed. For always and forever you are God.

You will need
A hula hoop (or any circular object)
A candle
An ice cube and a glove for handling
A glass of water
A fork

Introduction
Set pupils some impossible or almost impossible tasks, and ask why they would be impossible. Either you or the pupils could try doing these:

Light a candle with an ice cube.
Drink water with a fork.

Core material
Artists found they had an impossible task when they wanted to draw God. How can you draw someone who is invisible? Different artists solved this problem in different ways. Many artists drew symbols to represent God. A symbol is a type of sign. Teachers may wish to explain signs and use the ones provided on page 21. A sign gives us information in simple picture form. There are signs all around us: when you see a red cross, you know it means medical help. When you see a red circle and a cigarette, it means no smoking. Artists use special signs - we call them symbols - so that when people see them they think about God. One symbol artists drew for God was a circle.

Ask one pupil to demonstrate rolling the hula hoop. Hold it up. Christians use the circle as a symbol of God because they believe he has no beginning and no end. If this circle did have a beginning and an end you wouldn't be able to play with it. Take a large ball of wool. Hold one end. Ask a pupil to walk around the hall until they reach the end. You can knot the two ends and create a circle round the hall with children holding it at various points. As soon as it becomes a circle it has no beginning and no end. Christians believe God is eternal: that means he goes on forever - like the circle. He will always be there. Read the biblical material.

Prayer/Reflection
Pupils may like to trace a circle on the palm of their hand with a finger of the other hand as they listen to the prayer.

No beginning, No end. As we trace the circle, may we see it as a symbol of your presence.
Thank you for always being there.

Music suggestions
Teachers may like to play 'Windmills of your mind' by Noel Harrison (VTDMC80 EMI) for the pupils to enter the assembly.

'Oh Lord, all the world belongs to you.' A Year of Celebration, ed. J. Porter and J. Mc Crimmon (McCrimmons 1995)

'Love will never come to an end.' The Complete Come and Praise, comp. G. Marshall-Taylor (BBC 1990)

Biblical material

Psalm 139.7-12

Where could I go to be out of God's sight?
If I go to the highest heavens, you are there.
If I go to the depths of the earth, you are there also.
If I went to the farthest parts of the sea,
even there your hand would hold
me, guiding and protecting me.
The darkness does not hide
me from you,
for darkness is like daylight to
you.

You will need

Paper and pen
Hand paint, paper and hand wipes

Introduction

Ask pupils about all the good things we can
do with our hands. Pupil suggestions can be listed on
the paper. Look at some of the suggestions with pupils
and ask them to make their hands do some of the
things listed as you say them. Alternatively, a few pupils
could mime certain actions that hands could do.

Hands can work.

Hands can help others.

Hands can protect.

Hands can care.

Core material

Recap on the symbols section of the assembly on
pages 21 and 52. Ask one or two pupils to make hand
prints or draw round each other's hand, either on
paper or on an acetate which can be used on the over
head projector. Artists often used a hand as a symbol
of God. This does not mean God has hands. We use
the word 'hand' as a symbol of care when we offer to
'give someone a hand' with a job. We do not mean it
literally. With our hands, we can help others, and we
can show how we care. The hand of God was used to
express the Christian belief that God cares and acts.
The Bible talks about God holding people's hand. It is
a way of saying he cares. Read the biblical material.
Pupils can create movement to interpret this which
can be used while
the psalm is read as
part of the
reflection.

Prayer/Reflection

Pupils can look at their own hands and think about
the way they can show their care through them. Still
looking at their hands, they can listen to the prayer a
Christian might say.

*Every time we look at our hands, may we see them as a
symbol of your care.*
*Every time we look at our hands, may we see them as a
symbol of your work in Creation.*
*Every time we look at our hands, may we see them as a
symbol of your comfort.*
*Every time we look at our hands, may we see them as a
symbol of your power and protection.*

Music suggestions

'He's got the whole world in his hand.' The Complete
Come and Praise, comp. G. Marshall-Taylor (BBC 1990)

'Put your hand in the hand of the man from Galilee.'
Alleluya, comp. D Gadsby and J. Hogarth (A and C
Black Publishers Ltd. 1980)

Biblical material
Deuteronomy 6.4

Listen, O my people: the Lord your God is one Lord and you shall love him with all your heart, mind and strength.

You will need

A plastic number one (optional)
The words of the song written out

Introduction

Explain that today they are going to learn an old song called 'Green grow the rushes O.' It is a song that teaches numbers. We are going to learn the first verse which is about number one. Note: this can be developed into a round.

1)   I'll sing you one O.

2)   Green grow the rushes O.

1)   What is your one O?

2)   One is one and all alone and
        ever more shall be so.

The song can be sung by two groups. This old rhyme is actually about God. It says he is one, and always will be.

Alternative: Those who have no one able to play the piano or teach the song can introduce the assembly by talking about things which are unique: of which there is only one.

Core material

Recap on the explanation of symbols on pages 21 and 52 if necessary. The number one is a symbol of God. Christians believe there is only one God: there is no one else as powerful or as loving. Read the biblical material. Number one is also a reminder of the Christian belief that God should come first, for they believe he is the most important, the best.

With older pupils, you could try using metaphors to explain how Christians think of God as one and first in importance. 'If God were a record, he would be number one in the charts.' 'If God were a runner, he would be first past the tape.'

Prayer/Reflection

Ask pupils to think about what is important to them, then read the prayer which reflects a Christian's feeling about God. The plastic number one can be placed on an overhead projector to create a shadow.

You're the number one, the only one. The first, the highest and the best.
The rest come second.

Music suggestions

Teachers can play 'Simply the best' by Tina Turner (EMI TCESTUI) for the pupils to enter the assembly.

'How great is our God.' Junior Praise, comp. P. Horrobin and G. Leavers (Marshall Pickering 1986)

'All things bright and beautiful.' The Complete Come and Praise, comp. G. Marshall-Taylor (BBC 1990)

Green Grow The Rushes, O

I'll sing you One O, Green grow the rush-es, O. What is your one O? One is one and all a-lone and ev-er-more shall be so.

Biblical material
John 9.5; John 1.5

I am the Light of the World.

The light (Jesus) shone in the darkness and the darkness did not put it out.

You will need
Paper and pen
Several candles and matches
A tray of damp sand
A mirror
A clay pot or glass jar
Water

Introduction
Place a candle in damp sand and light it. Ask pupils about different ways of putting it out. You could blow it out, wet it, put a pot/jar over the top and starve it of oxygen. Try some of these with older pupils under safe conditions. Some things are easily put out, like the candles. Others are harder to extinguish.

Core material
Show the mirror and the candle. Ask what the difference is. The candle is a source of light, the mirror only reflects light. The mirror passes on the light it receives on its surface. Show how the mirror reflects light by reflecting a patch of light onto the wall behind you. Be careful not to shine it in pupils' eyes.

Christians call Jesus 'The Light of the World'. That does not mean he is shiny or bright. Light is a symbol of love, goodness, power and of being special (holy).

Christians believe that Jesus' goodness was a little like a strong light that is difficult to put out. Whatever people did, they could not 'put out' his love - not by hatred, injustice or even death - unlike our candles. Read the biblical material.

Christians call Jesus 'The Light of the World.' They believe that they should reflect, as a mirror, the light of Jesus' love to others. Use the mirror again and show how it reflects light. Just as a mirror catches light and passes it on, Christians believe they should pass on the love they receive from Jesus.

Prayer/Reflection
Place a candle in the damp sand and light it. Ask pupils to think about things that reflect light: mirrors, foil, shiny things. Place the mirror by the candle and create a reflection on the wall and read the Christian prayer.

Lord, your light shone and nothing put it out: not hatred, not injustice not even death.
Help us to be like mirrors that reflect your love in our world.
May we not be discouraged when we meet injustice and wrong.
Help us to treat such experiences as reminders of why the world needs the light of your love.

Music suggestions
'This little light of mine.' Junior Praise 1, comp. P. Horrobin and G. Leavers (Marshall Pickering 1986)

'There's a light.' Come and Praise Beginning, comp. G. Marshall-Taylor and D. Combes (BBC 1996)

Biblical material
See page 89 (Feeding the 5,000)

You will need
Blu Tak
A large piece jigsaw puzzle

Introduction
Take a large piece jigsaw puzzle and give different parts to different pupils. Ask them to guess the whole picture from what they have. Bring the pupils together and ask them to put the puzzle together on an upright board using Blu Tak to attach the pieces. How correct were they about the whole puzzle?

Core material
Read the biblical material. Christians believe that Jesus was someone very special: they believe he was God's Son. Jesus did things that made people think. After he had fed the five thousand people, Jesus deliberately went away: he left people to make up their own minds about who he was. His life was like a jigsaw puzzle. People saw lots of different bits: it was like having one or two pieces of a jigsaw puzzle and having to work out the whole picture. Some heard him teach and saw Jesus the teacher. Others saw Jesus the healer. Some saw Jesus the carer. Jesus left people to put the pieces of the jigsaw puzzle together themselves and work out who he was.

Prayer/Reflection
Enlarge the pieces on the photocopier and slowly put them up as the prayer is read. Explain that for Christians, the pieces of the jigsaw puzzle fit together to make Jesus the Son of God. This is how a Christian might respond:

Jesus the healer, Jesus the teacher, Jesus the miracle worker, Jesus the carer. Put them together and what have you got? More than a healer, more than a teacher, more than a miracle worker, more than someone who cared.

Music suggestions
'Fish and bread.' Feeling Good, P. Churchill (The National Society/Church House Publishing 1994)

'Bread for the World.' The Complete Come and Praise, comp. G. Marshall- Taylor (BBC 1990)

Biblical material

Matthew 22.15-22

One day, the religious leaders tried to get Jesus into trouble. They sent some of their followers to ask him about the taxes the people had to pay to the King. 'Master,' they said. 'Tell us - is it right for people to pay taxes to the King?'
Jesus knew that it was a trap. 'Bring me a coin,' he replied, and they brought one to him.
'Tell me, whose picture is on this coin?' asked Jesus.
'The King's head,' the religious leaders replied, feeling rather puzzled.
'Right,' said Jesus. 'Give what belongs to the King, to the King. But give what belongs to God, to God.'

You will need

Some coins and some Monopoly money

Introduction

Show a coin with the monarch's head. Explain that taxes are still collected from people for the government who rule the country. (Make sure that pupils do not confuse taxis and taxes.) In Jesus' time taxes were collected for the Roman King or Emperor (Caesar) who ruled Jesus' country. (You might want to show a map at this point). A short drama can be done by pupils or members of staff to explain the first century situation. They will need notices pinned to their fronts saying who they are, or they can introduce themselves to the audience.

Employee: Simeon Workalot
Employer: Marcus Paylittle
Tax man: Jonas Grabalot

Simeon: Thank goodness it's Friday, pay-day!

Marcus: Here are your wages, Simeon. Don't spend it all at once. **EXIT**
Simeon stops and adds it up.

Jonas: I'll take some of that! I'm collecting taxes for Caesar. *Jonas takes some money.* That's for the Roman roads we are building.
I'll have some more for the water works. *He takes some more.*

And the army. *Still more.*
Let's not forget the navy. *Even more.*

Simeon: Are you sure you have enough?

Jonas: No! There are the new towns we want to build and the Roman baths. *He takes even more money.* **EXIT**

Simeon: You would have thought Caesar had enough money of his own without having to take it from poor people like me! *He waves the few notes he has left.* **EXIT**

Core material

The Jewish people, like Simeon, hated paying taxes to the Roman King (Caesar). Jesus' enemies used this situation to try to trap him. Read the biblical material.

If Jesus had said, 'Pay taxes', the people would not have liked him. If he had said, 'Don't pay your taxes', he would have been in trouble with the King. Jesus did not tell people not to pay their taxes, but he didn't tell them to pay them either. He told people to give the King only what he has a right to ask. For example, 'If the King asks people to steal or do something wrong, don't do it.' Deciding what is right and wrong belongs to God, not the King.

Prayer/Reflection

Ask pupils to think about things it would be wrong for a king to ask a person to do.

Father we pray for the people who rule over us. We pray that they may be just and fair and only ask us to do those things which are right.

Music suggestions

'Jesus teach me.' Children's Praise, comp. P. Burt, P. Horrobin and G. Leavers (Marshall Pickering 1991)

'Your ways are higher than mine.' Junior Praise 1, comp., P. Horrobin and G. Leavers (Marshall Pickering 1986)

Biblical material

Matthew 7. 24-27

Once there were two men, and both wanted to build a house. The first man built his house on solid rock. It was hard work and it took time, but when the storms and the rains came, the house stood firm. The second man built his house on sand. The sand was easy to dig and the house was quickly built, but as soon as the storms hit and the rains came, the river rose and the house collapsed.

You will need

Some sand in a tray
Duplo or Lego in another tray
A small bucket of water
Paper and pens

Introduction

Discuss building with Lego and ask a few pupils to come and build a small house. One group can build a house on a high mound of sand in a tray. The other can build a house on a firm Lego base in another tray. Ask the pupils which would be the more secure. Test how secure the houses are by pouring water over them. The sand construction should topple. Ask pupils why one was more stable than the other.

Core material

Read the biblical material. During life, we all meet some trouble. Jesus likened this trouble to a storm.

With pupils draw some storm clouds and write on them some of the stormy troubles that we can face. Jesus said that a person who heard and obeyed his teaching was like a man who built his house on a rock. Christians believe that when the stormy troubles in life come, that person can stand firm. They don't just give up. Jesus said the man who built his house on sand was like someone who said they believed in Jesus but never actually obeyed his teaching.

Sometimes, Christians draw a symbol of the rock for the Church. This reminds Christians that the Church is made up of people who are friends of Jesus and are trying to put Jesus' words into action. Jesus is like the rock on which they build their lives. Just as the man built his house on a firm rock, so Christians believe that friendship with Jesus is like a rock that will stay firm when life gets stormy. They remember what Jesus said and did and try to put it into practice themselves.

Prayer/Reflection

Ask pupils to listen to the prayer or to think about putting words into action.

Father, thank you for the story of the house on the rock which reminds us that listening is not enough. Words have to be put into action.

Music suggestions

'Jesus is the rock.' A Year of Celebration, ed. J. Porter and J. McCrimmon (McCrimmons 1995).

The song below comes from East Africa. Divide the pupils into two groups. One rhythm follows the other in question and answer format. The Swahili version is in brackets. Practise clapping or stamping the rhythm first.

1) Who is the rock?　　2) The rock is Jesus, the rock

   (Mwamba Mwamba)　　(Mwamba ni Jesu Mwamba)

Adapted by Robin Walker from the song 'Mwamba'. Taken from World Praise ed. by D. Peacock and G. Weaver, Harper Collins Publishers Ltd. Used with permission.

Biblical material

Mark 4.35-41

One evening the disciples were crossing the Lake of Galilee and Jesus was with them in the boat. Without warning a great storm hit. The waves came over the side of the boat and the disciples, although experienced fishermen, were afraid. Jesus was so tired he was asleep in the back of the boat. The disciples woke him and said, 'Master don't you care that we are about to drown?' Jesus got up. He ordered the wind to stop with the words, 'Quiet, be still!' Suddenly the water was calm. The disciples looked at each other in amazement. 'Who is this man,' they said, 'that even the winds and the waves obey him?'

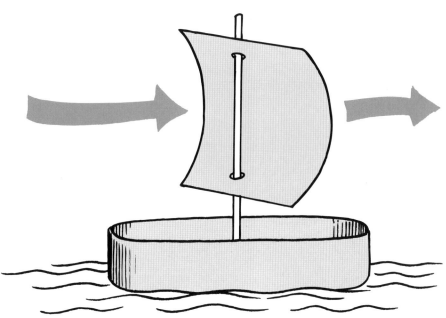

You will need

A shallow container that will float
Blu-Tak
A cocktail stick
Paper for a sail
A paper fan and a small battery powered fan
Container for water

Introduction

With the pupils make a boat with a sail and use the fan to make it move. Talk with pupils about the wind making the boat move and how sailing ships still use this form of power. The paper fan can be used to move the boat gently or the teacher can try creating a storm with a battery powered fan.

Core material

Read the biblical material. In the story, Jesus is with the disciples in the boat. The boat or ship became a symbol of the Christian Church. Christians believe Jesus goes with them through life, just as he was in the boat with the disciples when they were on the Lake of Galilee. The Church is the Christian community 'sailing' through life with Jesus as the captain.

The symbol on page 92 can be photocopied and enlarged or pupils might like to paint a large ship, HMS CHURCH prior to the assembly.

Christians often liken life to a sea journey. When we are born it is the beginning of a life's journey. It may be stormy in life, just as it can get stormy at sea. There may be troubles and problems but Christians believe they are never alone: Jesus is always there, just as he was in the boat during the storm on the lake. Christians also have other Christians (who make up the Church) for company on the journey. They do not sail on their own.

Prayer/Reflection

Ask pupils to close their eyes and imagine being in a ship. The water is calm and the breeze soft. The water gets a bit choppy and the wind blows cold. The prayer below can be read while they imagine this.

'Father, when the sea of life is calm we often forget you. When things start to get rough we remember. We feel like crying with the Breton fishermen, "O Lord, the sea is so great and my boat is so small." Help us to remember we are not alone. There are others with us travelling through life and you can steer the ship.'

Music suggestions

'With Jesus in the boat we can smile at the storm.' Junior Praise 1, comp. P. Horrobin and G. Leavers (Marshall Pickering 1986)

'Put your hand in the hand.' Alleluya, comp. D. Gadsby and J. Hogarth (A and C Black 1980)

Biblical material

Ephesians 2.14

Christ is our peace. He has destroyed the barrier of hatred that separated us and made us one.

You will need

An orange (shops often have scarred ones)
A globe
A knitting needle

Introduction

Aotearoa-New Zealand is on the opposite side of the world to the United Kingdom. Imagine this orange represents the world: if we mark where the United Kingdom is and push a knitting needle through the middle to the opposite side of the orange/world (teacher only), where it comes out would be roughly where Aotearoa- New Zealand is. Discard the orange after use. Show the globe and ask pupils to find the United Kingdom and Aotearoa-New Zealand. Below are a few facts about Aotearoa-New Zealand:

1) It takes a day and a night to fly there from Britain.

2) It is summer in Aotearoa- New Zealand - when it is winter here.

3) Aotearoa- New Zealand - has two languages, English and Maori.

4) It has 3.3 million people: 12% are of Maori descent.

5) Maoris are the original inhabitants of Aotearoa-New Zealand. European, particularly British, people came to settle in Aotearoa-New Zealand. In 1840, Christian missionaries successfully encouraged Queen Victoria to sign the Treaty of Waitangi which guaranteed Maori land and rights. Unfortunately, that treaty was later broken.

Core material

Maori Christians reflect in their Christian faith their pride in being Maori and their faith in Jesus. 'We have grasped Christianity with an unshakeable grip, because it makes sense to everything that is noble and good in being Maori.' (Maori elder). Although there has been bad feeling between the two communities over the breaking of the treaty, Maori Christians are one with non-Maori Christians as they share Jesus' message and work for justice in their own land, as this symbol shows. (The symbol can be enlarged on the photocopier).

The heart at the centre refers to God.

The two curls surrounding the heart are the two peoples of Aotearoa-New Zealand: Maori and Pakeha (non-Maori).

The large 'umbrella' curl over the top symbolises Christ who unites the two peoples.

The two sets of curls at the side that look like waves represent the troubles we all face in life.

Prayer/Reflection

Recap on the symbol. The prayer below can also be used.

We pray for the peoples of Aotearoa-New Zealand, for the healing of past wrongs, and for the present search for justice. May both the peoples serve you, each in their own way.

Music suggestions

'Every colour under the sun.' Come and Praise Beginning, comp. G. Marshall-Taylor and D. Coombes (BBC 1996)

'The ink is black.' Someone's Singing, Lord, comp. B. Harrop (A and C Black 1992)

You will need

A travel brochure
A suitcase
Items needed in a hot country

Introduction

This is part of a series of assemblies which will introduce pupils to different parts of the world. It may help to create a giant 'passport' with pages that can be filled in and 'stamped' every time you 'visit' a country. The assemblies on pages 60, 61 and 67 can be introduced this way. Explain that today, they are going to 'visit' El Salvador. It is many miles away in Central America. Ask pupils how you could get there. Explain that you have to cross an ocean. It is also a hot country. Ask the pupils what should go in the suitcase for such a country. Show your sun tan lotion for protection from the sun, your sun glasses, sun hat and other items needed for a hot country.

Core material

El Salvador is a small country about the size of Wales (show El Salvador on the world map). If we went to El Salvador we would see beautiful mountains and valleys. We would hear music (play some suitable music, see below) and we would hear people speaking Spanish.
Teach children a few Spanish words.

Hello = olà *(oh la)*   Good-bye = adios *(addy oss)*
Please = por favour *(porr fa vorr)*
Thank you = gracias *(grrarce ee ass)*

It sounds like a wonderful place for a holiday, but it is not safe for tourists! There is violence on the streets of El Salvador. Even the most beautiful places can be ruined by wrong. The people of El Salvador have known many years of ill-treatment, poverty and war. Many would think that the people of El Salvador would have given up hope, but the Christians of El Salvador believe in a God who 'walks' beside his people, even if they cannot see him. They believe that

Jesus is with them as they struggle against the wrong in their country and try to put it right.

Prayer/Reflection

Pupils can think quietly about the people of El Salvador. A people that want the same things as we do: to grow up in freedom, peace and safety with enough to eat, an education and people that love us. Teachers might like to read the following reflection and prayer:

The name El Salvador means 'The Saviour' or rescuer. Christians call Jesus the Saviour (or Rescuer).

This reminds the people of El Salvador that Jesus wants to rescue people from wrong.

In the cathedral, in the capital city of El Salvador, stands a statue of Jesus called 'Salvador del Mundo' which means 'Saviour of the World'.

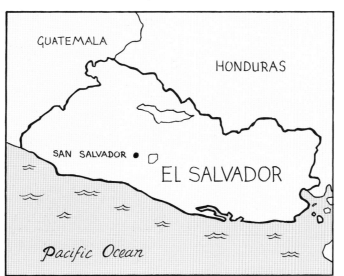

This reminds the people of El Salvador that Jesus cares for everyone, not just the people of El Salvador.

El Salvador, The Saviour. Salvador del Mundo, Saviour of the World.

Thank you, Father, for the example of so many of the people of El Salvador whose faith helps them face and fight poverty and wrong.

Music suggestions

Pupils might like to enter to some Central or South American Music such as: 'Rough Guide to the Music of the Andes' (The World Music Network RG NET 1009CD) or 'Music of the Andes' (Hemisphere 7243 8 28190 28)

'Jesus Christ is here.' The Complete Come and Praise, comp. G. Marshall-Taylor (BBC 1990)

'Jesus with us.' Rejoice 1, comp. A. White, A. Byrne and C. Malone (Harper Collins Religious 1993)

Note: *this assembly can be linked to the material on El Salvador on page 92.*

Biblical material

The Christmas story: Matthew 1.18 - 2.12; Luke 1.26-38; 2. 1-20

You will need

A map
Some Christmas decorations
Adverts for Christmas foods

Introduction

Encourage pupils to describe what they might do on Christmas Day and show the pictures. What would they eat and drink? What decorations would be used? Show pupils where Kenya is on the map. Read the account of a Christmas in Kenya.

Core material

On Christmas Day in Kenya, most Christians would eat beef, goat or chicken. This would be cooked with onions, tomatoes, carrots, peas and cabbage to make a stew. With it there would be chapattis and drinks such as Fanta or Coca Cola. Passionflower leaves and fresh flowers decorate the church. Children would be given sweets and biscuits, for the service might go on from nine in the morning until two in the afternoon, because there would be so much rejoicing. On Christmas Day many people confess their sins and receive forgiveness. This is like starting life with a clean slate. It's like being born anew with the baby Jesus.

Christmas is also a time of keeping promises. If a gift has been promised, Christmas is the time to keep that promise. One seven year old girl brought her foot size drawn on a piece of paper to church because she had been promised a pair of coloured wellington boots.

The emphasis is on celebration, being together and worship. Here is an account of the Christmas story in a Kenyan context by Andrew aged 10.

'As a rat my day starts when the sun goes down. One day I woke up in the evening and went looking for some food. A cat saw me and chased me into a Masai hut and I ran to the top of the haystack and looked to see where I was. I saw on my left a basket on the ground and some elephants and other animals looking into the basket. A bright light was shining in the door. As the cat had gone, I went outside to see what was shining. I looked up at the sky and saw a big star. Then I hurried back into the Masai hut and went to the other side of the basket. I saw a little baby lying in some hay. Near the baby was a man and a lady. Just then, some Masai shepherds entered the hut, each with a calf. One Bantu, one Nyamwezi and one Kikuyu chief came with beads, skins and ivory. They got on their knees saying, "Bwana, Bwana." (My Lord, My Lord). I couldn't see the little baby now because the chiefs had got in my way. As I scurried out, I wondered what all the excitement was; maybe the baby was special.'

Prayer/Reflection

This reflection comes from Uganda, a country near Kenya. Point out Uganda on the map.

'A few days before Christmas, we found out that a friend had no food in the house and both she and her family were hungry. On Christmas morning, the son of a student was taken ill, having been bitten by a dog. Thankfully we could help with the food and the young boy was successfully treated. These events made us think about Christmas. The message of Christmas is that Christ was born into a world of worry. We need to learn how to celebrate truly Christ's birth and also be open to the everyday problems of life. Only then will our celebration be real.' Based on a letter from Tudor and Nelleke Griffiths.

Music suggestions

'Our eyes have seen the glory.' Junior Praise, comp. P. Horrobin and G. Leavers (Marshall Pickering 1986)

'In Jesus' name.' A Year of Celebration, ed. J. Porter and J. McCrimmon (McCrimmons 1995)

With thanks to Martyn Payne and the Church Mission Society.

You will need
Your best clothes
Artificial flowers or ones made from
tissue paper
A clock

Introduction
If possible conduct this assembly
wearing your best clothes. Talk with
pupils about the time at which they
get up in the morning. Ask older
pupils to set the hands of the clock
for the time when they get up.
Have any of them ever got up
really early? On what
occasions might people
get up really early in
the morning? You
might like to arrange
a short mime by two
pupils, one acting as the
parent, the other as a child
reluctant to get up.

Core material
Some people get up really early on
Christmas Day because they want their presents. In
South India the Christians get up very early, about two
or three o'clock in the morning! They do this in order
to be at church really early to celebrate Jesus'
birthday, not because they want to open their presents
as soon as possible. Here is an account of Christmas
in South India.

'At Christmas, Christians in South India buy new
clothes, if they can, to wear for the Christmas service.
This is more important to them than giving presents.
The service on Christmas Day begins at 4 o'clock in
the morning. People have to get to church by three
thirty to get a seat. To get to the church people have
to walk through the cool darkness. To walk so early in
the morning, when everyone else is asleep, feels like
being a shepherd on the way to the manger. When
people get to church it is ablaze with lights. Everyone
is wearing their new clothes. The women and girls
have long thick strings of sweet smelling jasmine in
their hair. Some have roses and lilies too.

'Everyone sings as joyfully as they can, for it is the
birthday of Jesus, 'The Light of the World.' The service

ends at about six in the morning and
everyone comes out into the fresh air
to see the beautiful red sunrise in the
eastern sky. Later in the day, many
babies are brought to church to be
christened. Lots of babies are
christened on Christmas Day: they
are welcomed into the light of
God's family.'

Ask pupils if they can tell you what
Christians in South India do to
celebrate Christmas. Point out that
you are wearing your best
clothes and talk about other
occasions when you would
wear them. Demonstrate
on yourself, or on
another member of
staff or pupil, how
the flowers are worn.
Talk with the pupils about
times when they put on their
best clothes. What would the
girls put in their hair for a special
occasion? Christmas is really a
special occasion for Christians in India,
not because of the presents, but because it is Jesus'
birthday.

Prayer/Reflection
Ask pupils to close their eyes and think about the way
Christmas is celebrated in this country.

The prayer below can be said.

As Christmas approaches, may we remember the true
meaning of Christmas, for Christmas is not just about
presents: it is about the birth of a baby whom Christians
call 'The Light of the World'.

Music suggestions
Pupils might like to enter to Asian music such as 'Asia
Worships.' Mukti Dil -Aye (Kingsway KMC712)

'Christmas on the way.' Rejoice 1, comp. A. White
(Harper Collins Religious 1993)

'Many years ago.' Sing for Joy, S. Stevens (EMI Music
Publications 1980)

Information taken from Junior Link Letter by Mary Patterson: with thanks to
Martyn Payne of the Church Mission Society.

Biblical material
I John I.9

If we admit we have done wrong things, God has promised that he will forgive us and will make our lives right again. (paraphrased)

You will need
Ingredients of pancakes:- flour, eggs, milk, water, (Or the ingredients of bannocks: barley or oatmeal, currants if used)
Lemon and sugar
Vinegar
Paper 'pancakes'
Felt tips
(Note: bannocks can be substituted for pancakes in this assembly.)

Introduction
What special day is it today ? (Or ask what is special about the date of Shrove Tuesday.)

Talk about pancakes - who enjoys them? Which toppings do the children like?

One popular topping is lemon juice and sugar. What else do we need for pancakes?

Here are the ingredients (explain word if necessary). Show them to children, one at a time.

Leave the lemon hidden; bring out the vinegar. Are these ingredients correct? Vinegar would spoil the pancakes if we used it instead of lemon. It is a wrong ingredient. Substitute one of the ingredients for bannocks with a wrong, but safe, ingredient if demonstrating them instead of pancakes.

Core material
One of the ingredients was wrong. The pancakes/bannocks were fine until then! Christians believe that people's lives are like pancakes! A person's life can be good - until they add a wrong ingredient. Then that wrong ingredient can spoil life. Encourage the children to name things (wrong ingredients) which can spoil lives - such as lying, stealing, bad temper. Write some of these on the paper 'pancakes' - one to each 'pancake'.

Shrove Tuesday is the beginning of the part of the Church Year called Lent. For Christians, Lent is a time for looking at their lives, finding any wrong ingredients in them, and then getting rid of them so that they no longer spoil their lives. Christians believe that if they say sorry for the wrong things they have done, God will forgive them, and will help them not to do those wrong things again. (Read the biblical material.) They believe God will help them replace the wrong ingredients with the right ones. Hold up each 'pancake', and ask for the replacement ingredient to write on the other side. For example, replace lying with honesty.

Prayer/Reflection
Ask pupils to look at the paper 'pancakes' and focus on one wrong ingredient and its replacement, then listen to the prayer.

Dear Father, many things can spoil people's lives, things like lying, bad temper and selfishness. Thank you that you can help people to replace those wrong ingredients, so that their lives contain such things as honesty, generosity and patience.

Music suggestions
'It's hard to say I'm sorry.' Big Blue Planet, ed. J. Jarvis (Stainer and Bell Ltd. and Methodist Church Division of Education and Youth 1995)

'I'm sorry.' Feeling Good. by P. Churchill (The National Society/Church House Publishing 1994)

You will need

Chocolate and other luxury items given up during Lent
Large sheets of paper
Large, safe, felt-tipped pens
Blu-Tak
A cardboard box
Sellotape

Introduction

Write some mildly offensive words on one sheet of paper and talk about why it would be a good idea to give up some words.

Core material

Many Christians give up luxury foods for Lent. They might give up chocolate or sweets (show the chocolate). Some Christians give up certain words for Lent, but not because they are rude or upset people. The words Christians give up for Lent are joyful words which do not feel right to use in Lent because Lent is a sad time, a time when Christians think about the death of Jesus.

One of the words which is given up for Lent is 'Alleluia' which means 'Praise the Lord'. At Easter, Christians celebrate Jesus' resurrection (coming to life). Lots of Easter songs use the word 'Alleluia' so it is saved especially for Easter.

Tell the pupils they are going to listen to the word 'Alleluia' being sung. If possible, play them the 'Hallelujah Chorus' by Handel or 'Amen Alleluia' from *Many and Great* (Wild Goose Publications).

Write the word 'Alleluia' on a separate piece of paper in large letters. Leave some gaps between the letters. Tear the word 'Alleluia' into its four separate syllables and encourage the pupils to clap it or use simple percussion (page 17). Pupils can then try singing the South African song on page 90.

Some Christians write the word 'Alleluia' on a piece of paper, decorate it and hide it in a box until Easter. Ask pupils to help you do this. Write the word 'Alleluia' on a large sheet of paper and ask pupils to help you decorate it. This can be attached to a wall, and pupils can be decorating it with patterns and drawings of flowers while you recap on its meaning and remind them why some Christians do not use it during Lent. When the 'Alleluia' is decorated, fold it and place it in a box and seal it. Tell the pupils that it will stay in there until you do an Easter assembly.

Note: when you open the box during an Easter assembly, recap on this assembly quickly and remind them why the 'Alleluia' is in the box. Once again play the 'Hallelujah Chorus' and talk about why Christians feel like singing 'Praise the Lord' on Easter Sunday.

Prayer/Reflection

The 'Alleluia' song on page 90 can be used as a reflection if appropriate. This song comes from South Africa. *Come and Praise: Beginning* contains a version of this song.

Music suggestions

'Alleluia.' Come and Praise: Beginning, comp. G. Marshall-Taylor and D. Combes (BBC 1996)

'Alleluya.' Alleluyah! comp. D. Gadsby and J. Hogarth (A and C Black 1980)

'All creatures of our God and King.' A Time to Sing, ed. H. Clarke and P. Kneale (Macmillan 1984)

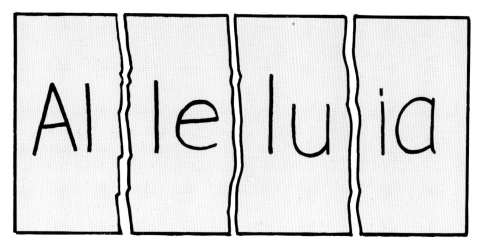

Biblical material

The story of Good Friday on page 90.

You will need

Some holly, and gloves for handling it
Party hats, party streamers etc.

Introduction

Talk about ways of celebrating. If you had really good news, how would you celebrate?

Some people go out and celebrate. Some people invite friends to a party. Show or demonstrate your party items: put on the hats, blow the whistles and throw the streamers. In the Middle Ages, people used to sing and dance to celebrate. The most joyful dances were called carols.

Core material

One carol people used to sing at Easter celebrations is all about holly. For Christians, it is a symbol of Easter, as well as Christmas. Ask pupils to think of words that describe holly (green, prickly etc). Holly is prickly and it reminds people of the crown of thorns which Jesus wore. It is a sad symbol, but Christians remember that Good Friday was not the end of the story. Christians believe Jesus came alive again on Easter Sunday and is still alive to be their friend. A long time ago, people celebrated Jesus' resurrection by dancing carols such as this carol about holly.

If appropriate, learn the carol. A few percussion instruments can be given out for accompaniment. If they can practise beforehand, some pupils might like to create a circular dance for the chorus.

Verses:

2. Now the holly bears a berry as green as the grass, and Mary bore Jesus, who died on the cross:

3. Now the holly bears a berry, as black as the coal, and Mary bore Jesus, who died for us all:

4. Now the holly bears a berry, as blood is it red, then trust we our Saviour, who rose from the dead:

Verse 1 and chorus are on the score.

Prayer/Reflection

Display some holly. Ask children to look at it, then to close their eyes and listen to the prayer.

Sharp prickles on a glossy leaf: a symbol of pain, like the thorn upon the rose. The sadness that comes before the joy. Holly.

Music suggestions

'Good Friday.' Rejoice I, comp. A. White, A. Byrne, C. Malone (Harper Collins Religious 1993)

'When from the sky.' The Complete Come and Praise, comp. G. Marshall-Taylor (BBC 1990)

'Christmas time.' Come and Praise Beginning, comp. G. Marshall-Taylor and D. Coombes (BBC 1996)

Sans Day Carol

Biblical material
Mark 14.43-16.15

On the Thursday night of Easter week, Jesus was arrested and all his friends left him. Alone he faced the judges on Friday, and alone he died. Some of his friends and family watched from beneath the cross, but they were powerless to help him.

Some friends buried the body of Jesus on Friday evening and they rolled a great stone in front of the tomb to seal it. When they buried Jesus, they buried their hopes too. They thought he was God's special King, but he was dead. On Saturday, they mourned their friend.

On the Sunday morning, some women went to the tomb to scatter sweet herbs on Jesus' body, as a last act of friendship. To their amazement, they found the tomb empty! Later, they met Jesus himself: he had risen from the dead. He had not left them alone.

You will need
Vinegar and a lemon
Chocolate and some sugar
A black cloth
An icon or enlarge the drawing

Introduction
Ask pupils about sweet and sour tastes. Show the four items of food and ask them to select which ones are sweet and which are sour. Ask which ones are associated with Easter. We tend to associate chocolate with Easter Day as many people have Easter eggs.

There are, however, other foods eaten over the Easter period. In some countries, sour foods are used on Good Friday because they are sharp and bitter and remind people of the sharp pain and bitter suffering of Jesus. Sweet foods are eaten on Easter Day as a celebration of Jesus rising from the dead.

Core material
Cyprus is an island in the Mediterranean Sea. (You may wish to show pupils a map at this point or use the passport idea from page 61). Its population is largely Greek, though there is also a Turkish population in the north. Explain that icons are special paintings used in some churches. Demonstrate putting the cloth on the icon. (Small icons are often available from Christian book shops.)

During Holy Week all icons are covered in black cloth. On the Thursday before Good Friday, some people taste vinegar as a reminder of Jesus' bitter suffering. Girls prepare garlands of flowers for the following day, Good Friday. Good Friday is the day when people remember Jesus' death. Boys and girls dress in white. A special wooden structure is carried though the streets. Inside is an icon of Jesus. The structure is decorated with flowers and herbs and at night it is guarded by older women.

On Easter Sunday the celebrations begin. The black cloths are removed from the icons, the candles are lit and the people all shout, 'God has risen'. At home, special Easter food is shared and fireworks lit.

Prayer/Reflection
Place the vinegar, lemon, sugar and chocolate on the table. Ask pupils to try to remember the taste of vinegar or lemons. Now ask them to try and remember what chocolate tastes like.

The sharp taste of lemon bites on the tongue.
Chocolate melts in the mouth.
As we remember the different foods,
may they remind us of the bitterness of suffering
and the sweet taste of joy.

Music Suggestions
Pupils can enter to some Greek music such as 'Zorba's Dance', Bouzouki Magic (CD. Castle Communications).

'All in an Easter garden.' The Complete Come and Praise, comp. G. Marshall-Taylor (BBC 1990)

'Jesus lives again.' Feeling Good, by P. Churchill (The National Society/Church House Publishing 1994)

Biblical material
John 20.1-18

Mary Magdalene, one of Jesus' followers, did not know what to do. She had come early to the tomb where Jesus' body was - but the great stone blocking the door had been moved! She had fetched Peter and John and they had gone into the tomb. They said his body had gone, and they rushed off to tell the others! But she stayed in the garden. She was very unhappy. They had killed Jesus and now they had taken his body! She realised that a man was standing near to her. 'It must be the gardener,' she thought. Wiping her eyes, she turned to him and said, 'Please tell me where you have put him.'

And the man said, 'Mary!'

Then Mary knew that this was Jesus himself. He was alive! She remembered how he had shouted, 'I've done it!' as he died on the cross, and she realised that he had known all along that he must die. He had died to save them - and here he was, alive again.

You will need
An orange
A plank of wood
Some books
An empty Easter egg box (optional)

Introduction
Give pupils a number of containers and boxes to open. Before they open them ask them what they might contain. The boxes can be gift wrapped, but all of them should be empty. If you can, buy an Easter egg, (eat the chocolate if you wish!) and reconstruct the foil so that it does not look empty. Ask a pupil to unwrap the Easter egg. Explain that finding something empty is often a disappointment, but the Easter story is about finding something empty and it being a good surprise.

Core material
In Dunstable some people have a very unusual custom. They get up on Easter morning and they take some oranges and go to Dunstable Downs (hills). The oranges are then rolled down the hill. The orange is a reminder of the stone that sealed the tomb (grave) of Jesus after he had been buried. Listen to the Bible story. The orange is rolled to remind Christians that the stone was rolled away and the tomb was empty: Jesus was not there. They believe he rose from the dead: death was not the end. The sadness of Good Friday was turned into the joy of Easter Sunday.

Prayer/Reflection
Listen to some Easter Sunday music. Think about the ways the composer has expressed Christian joy such as : 'Let us rejoice' from Cavelleria Rusticana by Pietro Mascagni (Deutche Grammophon 419 257-2) or 'Christ the Lord has Risen again' arranged by John Rutter (Te Deum Collegium Records COLCD112).

Music suggestions
'Now the green blade rises.' or 'All in an Easter garden.' The Complete Come and Praise, comp. G. Marshall-Taylor (BBC 1990)

'Jesus lives again.' Feeling Good, by P. Churchill (National Society/Church House Publishing 1994)

You will need
A number of coloured scarves

Introduction
Ask pupils to imagine that they have been invited to a special celebration. What would they wear? If possible wear your best clothes that day and explain why you chose them.

Core material
Easter is a special celebration for Christians, when they celebrate Jesus rising from the dead. Christians sometimes wear their best clothes to church. This is an account of how some Christians celebrate Easter in Zaire, a country in central Africa. The story is by Bena, Mokuba, Ipolu and Mpia-Mompanghe (Mom-pan-gay).

'Easter day is good because Jesus rose from the dead. The night before Easter we see a film called 'The death of Jesus.' It is a very good film but it makes us unhappy to see Jesus crucified. On Sunday the church is decorated with beautiful flowers, pictures, statues and crosses. We put on white clothes and the choirs put on head scarves (show the scarves and how they are tied) and dance with candles (do not try this!). Young people are baptised. When church is finished we have a feast; we eat beef, rice, cassava leaves and beans. We drink Coca Cola. All day long there is religious music at church.'

Prayer/Reflection
Ask pupils to think about things they celebrate while they listen to the Zairean prayer. Arrange for some pupils to practise the drum solos beforehand.

I shall sing a song of praise to God:
Strike the chords upon the drum. (drum solo)
God who gives us all good things -
Strike the chord upon the drums. (drum solo)

Music suggestions
Pupils can enter to African Christian music such as 'Bwana Asifiwe' or 'Kagando' (Available from Tear Fund, 100 Church Road, Teddington, Middlesex TW11 8QE.)

'Children, join the celebration.' Junior Praise 2, comp. P. Burt, P. Horrobin and G. Leavers (Marshall Pickering 1992)

Pupils can learn this joyful song from Zaire. It is often accompanied with dance. The words mean 'Jesus he is here with us, Hallelujah.' They are pronounced phonetically keeping the vowel sounds short.

Ye-su a-ja-li a-wa. Ye-su a-ja-li a-wa, Ye-su a-ja-li a- wa na-bi - so; Ye-su
a-ja-li a-wa, Ye-su a-ja-li a- wa, Ye-su a-ja-li a-wa na- bi - so.
Al-le-lu-ja, al - le-lu-ja, al-le-lu-ja na Ye- su,
Al-le-lu-ja, Al - le-lu-ja, al-le-lu-ja na Ye - su.

Prayer (extract) reproduced by permission of Hodder and Stoughton Ltd. From 'An African Prayer Book' by D. Tutu (1995). With thanks to Martyn Payne of the Church Mission Society for information on Zaire and the song.

Biblical material

John 16.7

Just before he died, Jesus told his disciples: 'I am going to leave you, but don't worry, it is for your own good. Unless I go away, the Holy Spirit will not come to you. But if I go, then I will send him to you.'

You will need

Recording of the opening of News at Ten (optional)

Introduction

People in stories and on television often say, 'I have some good news and some bad news.' Or 'Do you want the good news first or the bad news?' Have the children ever heard this on television? Give them some examples of 'good news/bad news'. These can be based on current events in the school, or you could use these examples. Pupils might like to make their own suggestions for good news/bad news.

'I have some good news and some bad news. The good news is that you will only have one lesson tomorrow. The bad news is that it will last from 9.00 o'clock until 3.30!'

'Good news! There is going to be a special school meal for everyone today. Bad news! It's going to be dry bread!'

The good news is that there is going to be a programme on at 10.00 o'clock with all your favourite stars in (such as....) The bad news is that none of you will be allowed to watch it!'

Core material

Jesus had some bad news for his disciples one day. They had spent three years travelling around the country with him. They had learned a lot from his teaching, and they had seen him do many amazing things. But then he told them, 'I am going to leave you very soon.' They were upset: they didn't want their friend to go. He told them that he was going back to live with his Father, God. 'But,' he said, 'I have some good news for you, too. In fact, it is good that I am going to leave you.' They were puzzled. How could it be good? Jesus explained, 'If I leave you and go back to my Father, then I will be able to send a new friend to you. He will be a wonderful friend to you, because he will never leave you, and he will stay with you, wherever you go.' Jesus was talking about the Holy Spirit. He told the disciples that the Holy Spirit would soon come to them - but this would only happen after he had left them.

(Note: the Holy Spirit is the way Christians refer to God as the real, but invisible, friend.)

Later on, they realised that Jesus was right. It was very good news that the Holy Spirit was going to stay with them! Sometimes we hear bad news that turns into good news later on. Moving to a new school or a new class seems like bad news to us. But later we see that the move has brought us new friends and new things to learn and do. Can you think of anything else that seemed all bad news at first, but changed later?

Prayer/Reflection

Ask pupils to reflect on a time when they heard bad news but it turned out to be good. They can do this whilst listening to the opening of 'News at Ten'. The prayer below can also be read.

Dear Lord, the disciples heard some bad news from Jesus. But later they realised that it was really good news! Help us to remember that some bad news can turn into good news for us too, even though it seems bad at the time.

Music suggestions

'Jesus' friends were looking up.' Children's Praise, comp. P. Burt, P. Horrobin and G. Leavers (Marshall Pickering 1991)

'Great news.' Rejoice 1, comp. A. White, A. Byrne and C. Malone (Harper Collins Religious 1993)

Biblical material

John 14.16

Jesus said, 'God will give you another Helper who will stay with you for ever.'

You will need

A fan (electric)
A match and some water

Introduction

How would you describe paddling in the sea? Or a thunderstorm? Or what it feels like to swallow ice-cream? Ask pupils to try to describe these things. Some things are easy to describe, but others are difficult! We sometimes use word-pictures to help us. We could say, 'The water was as cold as ice' or 'The thunder sounded like a great drum' or 'The ice-cream slithered down my throat like a slimy slug'!

These word pictures help other people understand what we are describing. Can you think of some word pictures to describe the following items? Pouring rain: thick fog: the taste of lemon juice: cold feet. You can start the descriptions: Fog as thick as.... Lemon as sharp as....

Christians found it hard to describe the Holy Spirit, too, so they used word-pictures to help them. They said, 'This is what the Holy Spirit is like,' and used things that other people would know and understand. Listen to the story of what happened when the Holy Spirit first came to the disciples.

Core material

Jesus had told the disciples to stay in Jerusalem until the Holy Spirit, God the invisible friend, came to them. They often met together to talk about Jesus and to think about all that he had told them about the Holy Spirit. Jesus had said that the Spirit would stay with them for ever, and would teach them, just as Jesus himself had done. The Spirit would be their friend, comforting them when they were sad, and helping them in everything they did. One day, as they talked together, they heard what seemed like a great strong wind rushing through the room. They looked round at each other in astonishment, and saw what seemed like flames, coming down through the air, until each one rested above a disciple. They realised that this was it - the Holy Spirit had arrived, and had come to live with each one of them. They were so full of joy that they started to shout and sing praises to God, to thank him for this great gift.

Other people heard this singing, and came to find out what was happening. Peter told them everything, explaining that Jesus was the Son of God, and that he was now alive again. He told them about the Holy Spirit who had just come to live with them. Many people listened to Peter, and became followers of Jesus themselves because of what they heard.

The disciples saw and heard the Holy Spirit as a wind and as flames. They were not in any danger! Wind and fire are powerful. Seeing and hearing wind and fire was a way of showing the disciples that the Holy Spirit is powerful to help. Wind and fire are like the word pictures we used early on in the assembly: they are a way of helping people understand.

Prayer/Reflection

Turn on a fan (adult only) and ask pupils to think about the power of the wind. Light a match under safe conditions. Ask pupils to think about the positve power of fire (warmth, cooking, power to move machines). The prayer below can also be read.

Thank you, Father, that the Holy Spirit came just as Jesus had promised. Thank you that he cares for people, and looks after them, just as Jesus said that he would.

Music suggestions

'May your loving Spirit.' Big Blue Planet, ed. J. Jarvis (Stainer and Bell Ltd. and Methodist Church Division of Education and Youth 1995)

'Pass it on.' Rejoice 1, comp. A. White, A. Byrne and C. Malone (Harper Collins Religious 1993)

Biblical material
1 Corinthians 11.23-25

On the night before he died, Jesus took the bread and gave thanks to God. He broke it and said, 'This is my body which is broken for you, do this to remember me.' He also took the cup and said, 'This is the new agreement in my blood, whenever you drink this wine, remember me.'

You will need
A picture of the earth from space (optional). The one provided can be enlarged or copied onto acetate.

Introduction
Ask pupils for a number of 'firsts'. Adjust the questions to the age and ability of the pupils.

Example:

Who was the first man on the moon? (Neil Armstrong, 1969)

With younger pupils, hold some very quick competitions: the first person to sit up straight, the first person to put their hand up, etc.

Show the picture of the earth from space. Bread and wine were the first foods to be eaten on the moon and they were not just any bread and wine, they were the special bread and wine that many Christians use to remember Jesus' death. Christians take a tiny sip of wine and a small piece of bread (or sometimes just one of these) at a special meal. The meal is called by different names. Some call it Breaking of Bread or the Lord's Supper. Others call it Communion or Eucharist.

Core material
'On the day of the moon landing, we awoke at 5.30 a.m., Houston time. Neil and I separated from Mike Collins in the command module. Our powered descent was right on schedule. With only seconds' worth of fuel left, we touched down at 3.30 p.m. ...Now was the time for Communion. So I unstowed (unpacked) the elements (bread and wine) in their flight packets. I put them and the scripture (Bible) reading on the little table in front of the abort guidance-system computer. Then I called Houston. "Houston, this is Eagle. This is LM Pilot speaking. I would like to request a few moments' silence. I would like to invite each person listening in, wherever and

whomever he may be, to contemplate for a moment the events of the past few hours and to give thanks in his own individual way." '

'For me, this meant taking Communion. In the blackout, I opened the little plastic packages which contained bread and wine. I poured wine into the chalice (cup) my parish (local Christians at home) had given me. In the one-sixth gravity of the moon, the wine curled slowly and gracefully up the cup. It was interesting to think that the very first liquid ever poured on the moon, and the first food eaten there, were consecrated elements (bread and wine).'

(Buzz Aldrin, one of the first astronauts on the moon).

Prayer/Reflection
Play the music from the film Apollo 13 or Space Odyssey. Ask pupils to think about moments that have been very special for them, and about this special moment for Buzz Aldrin.

Music suggestions
'5,4,3,2,1, and Zero' and 'God who put the stars in space.' Someone's singing, Lord, B. Harrop (A and C Black 1992)

Note: teachers may wish to adapt the quotation from Buzz Aldrin for younger pupils.

Reproduced from 'The Liturgy of Life' with the permission of the National Christian Education Council.

You will need

Some canned or dried food, and jam
Sweet corn (fresh if possible or a tin)
Some vegetables (optional)
Sun flower oil (optional)
12 cards - with the instructions below

Introduction

If we want food we can just pop down to the shops. Demonstrate buying food with the pupils. They can act a scene in a shop. This is not so in all parts of the world. Many people have to rely on what they can grow themselves. There are shops, but you need money to buy goods. Money comes from selling crops. If the crops fail, people can be left without food and money.

Core material

Ikengeza (Ih ken gay za) is a typical East African village in Tanzania. We are going to play a harvest game using people for the pieces. People in Ikengeza grow maize (sweet corn), sunflower seeds (for oil) and vegetables. Place a cob or tin of sweet corn, sunflower oil and vegetables on a table, a suitable distance (about 6-8 'paces') from the pupils who will act as pieces. The 'paces' can be marked with hoops or something similar. The pupils select at random from the pack of cards which move them forward and backward. The aim is to reach the food, the harvest.

Note: pupils never go backwards beyond the starting point.

(You will need 12 cards each with one of these sentences written on it.) Shuffle the pack of cards.

1) You get malaria. Back two paces
2) Water is short. Back one pace.
3) Cattle eat some of your crops. Back two paces.
4) Insects attack your crops. Back one pace.
5) Fungus attacks your crops. Back one pace.
6) Your son is sick and cannot help on the farm. Back two paces.
1) Your crops are doing well. Forward one pace.
2) You manure your crops. Forward one pace.
3) The rains arrive on time. Forward one pace.
4) You get a new hoe. Forward two paces.
5) You sell some crops at market. Forward two paces.
6) You buy extra land. Forward two paces.

As you can see, growing crops is a risky business - there are many dangers for the young plants and many difficulties for the farmers.

Prayer/Reflection

Ask pupils to think about the very ordinary foods which they take for granted. The prayer from Kenya can also be used.

Thank you very, very much;
my God, thank you.
Give me food today,
food for my sustenance every day.
Thank you very, very much.

Music suggestions

Pupils can enter to African music such as that on the tapes Bwana Asifiwe or Kagando (Tear Fund).

'First the seed and then the rain' and 'Always remember, never forget.' Big Blue Planet, ed. by J. Jarvis (Stainer and Bell and Methodist Church Division for Education and Youth 1995)

NOTE: The information above is adapted from the Ikengeza board game. An Ikengeza board game (junior), a leaflet called 'Food' suitable for infants and the music tapes can be purchased from Tear Fund, 100 Church Road, Teddington, Middlesex TW11 8QE.   Prayer taken from 'An African Prayer Book' by D. Tutu (Hodder and Stoughton 1995).

You will need
Any items from the Thanksgiving dinner (optional)
Paper
Large felt tipped pens

Introduction
Ask pupils what they would have if they were to have a special meal. Create a menu. For example:

Special Menu

Chicken
Roast potatoes
Peas and carrots
Gravy

Strawberry ice-cream

Core material
On the fourth Thursday in November, Americans celebrate Thanksgiving. In Canada, Thanksgiving is held on the second Monday in October.

Thanksgiving was first celebrated in 1622. Puritan Christians had left England in order to found a colony in America where they could live and worship in freedom. They arrived in November, which was far too late to plant crops before winter so the Puritan settlers had to face their first bitter winter, with little food. Nearly half the settlers died during that first winter. As soon as spring came, seeds were planted.

The Puritans were saved by the Amerindians who showed them how to plant corn (maize), pumpkin and sweet potato. They reaped their first harvest in the autumn and the leader of the settlers, William Bradford, declared a day of thanksgiving and prayer. Wild turkey may have been eaten, and the women gathered nuts and ground them with cornmeal to make bread. Wild plums and watercress turned it into a simple feast. If you have any of the items which make up a Thanksgiving dinner, show them to the pupils.

Today, a traditional Thanksgiving dinner consists of:

Corn bread
Turkey
Cranberry sauce
Pumpkin pie
Sweet potatoes

Create a Thanksgiving menu to place alongside the other menu.

Prayer/Reflection
Thanksgiving is a time when the people of North America say 'Thank you' to God. Any meal can be turned into a Thanksgiving meal simply by people being thankful.

As we remember those early settlers, we remember that they survived because they were helped by the Amerindians. As we eat our food, we are reminded to be thankful for the work that went into producing it and the care that went into preparing it. Although Thanksgiving may not be a festival we celebrate, may we turn each of our meals into a thanksgiving by being thankful.

Music suggestions
'The sharing bread.' The Complete Come and Praise, comp. G. Marshall-Taylor (BBC 1990)

'Always remember, never forget.' Big Blue Planet, ed. J. Jarvis (Stainer and Bell Ltd and Methodist Church Division for Education and Youth 1995)

You will need
Some fruit to 'auction'
Paper
Pens
A party invitation

Introduction
Show a party invitation and ask pupils about invitations they have sent or received. Draw two columns on the sheet of paper labelled WHEN and WHY. Ask pupils for suggestions of occasions when we have parties and why. Write their suggestions under the appropriate columns.

Core material
Harvest is a special celebration for many Christians. People bring food to church and have a special service. Sometimes they have a Harvest supper and a Harvest party as well. Later, the food is taken to those who need it, or it is auctioned and the money given to charity. Demonstrate an auction for the pupils by auctioning some fruit, using other members of staff and pupils as bidders. *Note: money does not have to be used.*

Harvest is like a 'Thank you' party. It is a time when Christians say 'Thank you' to God for the food which grows. Harvest celebrations, like those described above, only started in Queen Victoria's reign. Before that, only the workers who had been involved in getting the harvest in were given a Harvest Home supper by the farmer. It was not a religious celebration. Flora Thompson wrote about Harvest Home in her book *Lark Rise to Candleford*.

'...The last load was brought in, with a nest of merry boys' faces among the sheaves on the top, and the men walking alongside with pitchforks on shoulders. As they passed along the roads they shouted:

'Harvest home! Harvest home! Merry, merry, merry,

harvest home!'

and women came to their cottage gates and waved....and the farmer came out followed by his daughters and maids with jugs and bottles and mugs, and drinks were handed round amidst the general congratulations. Then the farmer invited the men to his Harvest Home dinner...'

There was, however, no celebration that thanked God for the harvest. Two vicars from the West Country, R.S. Hawker and G. Denison, decided to do something about this. They started their own Harvest celebration. They had a parade, and they decorated the church with flowers and fruit. There was a service followed by a Harvest supper which all the people of the village could attend. The new Harvest celebrations quickly caught on and became one of the most popular services of the year.

Prayer/Reflection
Christians say 'Thank you' to God for food at harvest time. Even if food is bought at the local shop, they believe it is God who makes things grow. This poem expresses that belief.

Before the loaf is the snowy flour,
Before the flour the mill,
Before the mill the sun, the shower,
The wind and our Father's will. (adapted)

Music suggestions
'Great News.' Rejoice 1, comp. A. White, A. Byrne and C. Malone (Harper Collins Religious 1993)

'For micro chips, for oven chips.' Big Blue Planet, ed. J. Jarvis (Stainer and Bell Ltd and Methodist Church Division for Education and Youth 1995)

Prayer reproduced from 'Celebrating Harvest' with the permission of the National Christian Education Council.

Extract from 'Larkrise to Candleford' by Flora Thompson used by permission of Oxford University Press (1945).

You will need

A sponge cake and candles
The picture of the fisherwife (enlarged or on acetate) -optional

Introduction

If you use this assembly for Harvest Festival, ask pupils what items people would bring to a Harvest service. In parts of Scotland and England, instead of making a display of fruit and vegetables, people display fish and celebrate the 'harvest of the sea'. Fisherman's Walk Festivals take place in some towns and villages in Scotland. At these festivals, women in traditional dress walk in procession carrying dolls dressed in similar costumes. Show the picture if you have one. Every time we eat fish and chips we need to remember that we eat the 'harvest of the sea' as well as the 'harvest of the land'. It is important to remember the men and women who work in the fishing industry and who bring us our food. For those on the boats, it is a difficult, and sometimes dangerous, job.

Alternative introduction

Light the candles and sing 'Happy Birthday'. Ask the pupils whose birthday it is. Tell them it is an organisation not a person. Using mime, give pupils some clues about the people the organisation helps. In 1996, The Royal National Mission to Deep Sea Fishermen was one hundred years old. Now it is — (add correct age, depending on when you do this assembly). The Mission is a Christian organisation founded to help deep sea fishermen.

Core material

One hundred years ago, many of the people who worked the fishing boats were orphans from the slums and workhouses of Victorian Britain. Life on the boats was tough and hard and filled with danger. Visits from the Mission staff were sometimes the only care these boys received.

Deep sea fishermen still face dangers as they fish for the food we eat, though conditions are better and fishing is much safer now. When we eat fish and chips, we need to remember and say 'Thank you' inside for the people who spend their lives catching fish. Deep sea fishermen have to spend long periods of time away from home, and while they are away their families have to cope on their own. The Mission tries to look after both the fishermen and their families.

The Mission provides practical help in emergencies as well as day to day support. If there is a rescue, the Mission provides food, warm clothes and a bed for those rescued. If there is a tragic accident, the Mission staff support the family. Here is one story about the Mission's work.

One night, a fishing boat went down in the Bristol Channel. The owners contacted the Mission who immediately set about finding all the relatives of the fishermen who were missing and possibly drowned. They did not want the families to have the shock of hearing about the tragedy on the television. There was not much time, the reporters had already heard about the accident. The Mission staff swung into action. The families were spread across the country and even in Australia, but by the time the story appeared on the news all the families had been told and received support. The Mission maintained contact with the families and also gave financial support where it was needed.

Prayer/Reflection

Play the tune to ' Eternal Father, strong to save' and explain that it is the fishermen/sailors' hymn. Pupils can silently say thank you for those engaged in the fishing industry; or you can read the prayer.

Plaice, mackerel, haddock and cod,
These are the fish we eat, O God.
For prawn and shrimp, sardines on toast,
Praise Father, Son and Holy Ghost.

Music suggestions

'Eternal Father, strong to save.' A Time to Sing, ed. H. Clarke and P. Kneale (Macmillan 1990)

'We thank you Lord.' The Complete Come and Praise, comp. G. Marshall- Taylor (BBC 1990)

Information adapted from 'Net Work': with thanks to The Royal National Mission to Deep Sea Fishermen.

'Fish-Harvest' from 'Prayers for Children' (National Society/Church House Publishing, 1993) is © Christopher Herbert and is reproduced by permission.

Biblical material

Galatians 6.10

Whenever we have a chance, let us do good to all people.

You will need

A pound and some items it will buy
Paper and pens
Monopoly money

Introduction

Hold up a pound coin and ask what it will buy, or bring in some items it could buy. A pound could buy four bars of chocolate, three fizzy drinks or one lottery ticket.

Core material

Create two 'families' each containing five people: three adults and two children in each: Mum, Dad, a grown up daughter or son and two children. In 'family' A, the adults earn fifty pounds a month but have no savings. In 'family' B, the adults earn five pound a month and have fifty pounds savings. The teacher hands them out their month's wages using monopoly money. The teacher holds onto any savings.

On two large sheets of paper, one for each family, the teacher writes the headings: food, clothes, education (this has to be paid for directly in many parts of the world). Each family divides the money they have for a month between the three categories. The amounts can be written up or the money can be pinned to the paper. They do not have to divide it equally. When they have done this, break the news that they also have to pay for health care (doctors, medicines etc.). Here is what different amounts of money will buy for one person:

One pound a month (level 1 health care)	poorly run health centres but no effective medicines and no emergency treatment
Two pound a month (level 2 health care)	well run health centres some essential medicines a vaccination programme but no emergency treatment
Ten pound a month (level 3 health care)	well run health centres ten essential medicines a vaccination programme but no emergency treatment
Fifty pound a month (level 4 health care)	good all-round health care good care of mothers and babies good vaccination programme good emergency service

Ask the 'families' what they will give up to pay for health care. Will they use their savings? Will they buy health care for all the family or only one or two members? What sort of health care could they afford? Money matters, as you can see from these two families. That is why the Bible talks about using it to make a difference to other people's lives (read the biblical material). Often we hear about the poverty in the world and feel helpless, yet just a pound can make a difference. A pound is what many adults spend on a lottery ticket!

Prayer/Reflection

Pupils can listen quietly while the prayer is read.

Father, we often feel helpless in the face of world poverty. We feel we can do little to change the situation. Help us to focus on what we can do, and the difference we can make.

Music suggestions

'Care for one another.' Children's Praise, comp. P. Burt, P. Horrobin, and G. Leavers (Marshall Pickering 1991)

'When your Father made the world.' The Complete Come and Praise, comp. G. Marshall-Taylor (BBC 1990)

With thanks to Jubilee 2000, PO Box 100, London SE1 7RT. Information adapted from 'The Debt Cutter's Handbook.' edited by I. Hanson.

You will need

Some vegetables
Foil
A glass photograph frame (optional)
A piece of black card and a piece of white card
A desk lamp

Introduction

Start with a science experiment, though this can be omitted for special needs pupils. Shine the light over the white and black card. Ask pupils which one they think will heat up first. While you are waiting for these to heat up, show the vegetables and ask how you could cook them. Where would you get the heat? If you had no gas or electricity, what could you do? Explain that, in many countries, people cook using wood as a source of heat.

Go back to the card and ask pupils to test which one is warmer (turn the light off first). Explain that white reflects (bounces away) heat and black absorbs (collects) it. This is the story of how some Christians used science to solve a problem.

Core material

Wars often leave people homeless. Refugees leave their own country for safety and may have to shelter in special camps in another country. The refugees have to chop down trees in order to survive, for they need fires to cook their food. Soon the forests around the camps become devastated, and people have to walk farther and farther for wood. The land takes years to recover.

In Christian supported workshops in Pakistan, small solar ovens have been developed; they are the size of a small suitcase. The ovens have an aluminium lid (show foil) that reflects the sunlight onto a glass (show glass frame) inner lid. The glass concentrates the sunlight (makes it hotter). The black pots used to cook the

food absorb the heat, and in two hours the meal is cooked. The design has been so successful that the United Nations have asked to use the design in other refugee camps. Now people can eat and the forests are protected.

Often, we hear of disasters and wars in the news. We do not always hear the good news. It is easy to focus on the things that we are not thankful for and think there is nothing to be happy about. This is only one good news story amongst many. The bad news is not the whole news.

Prayer/Reflection

The prayer below can be used if appropriate.

We thank you, Father, for scientists-
Men and women who explore the wonders of your world.
We pray that they may use their knowledge in the service of others.

Music suggestions

'Great News.' Rejoice 1, comp. A. White, A. Byrne and C. Malone (Harper Collins Religious 1993)

'Sad, puzzled eyes.' The Complete Come and Praise, comp. G. Marshall- Taylor (BBC 1990)

Information taken from Tear Times, produced by Tear Fund, 100 Church Road, Teddington, Middlesex TW11 8QR

Biblical material
Micah 6.8

What does God ask you to do? He asks you to be fair to others, to love them, even beyond what they deserve, and to walk humbly with your God through life.

You will need
Kettle
Tea
Cup and saucer
Teapot
Milk
A 1 kilogram weight
Sugar (optional)
A small leaf (make sure it is a safe variety to handle)

Introduction
Make a cup of tea and ask pupils what goes into it. They should be able to talk you through the process but you should actually make the tea. Most of us know what makes a cup of tea, but there are hidden ingredients in some tea. We are going to find out about some of these.

Core material
Imagine a tea picker from Sri Lanka - we will call her Ashika. She rises at four to fetch water and feed her family. After that, she walks to the tea plantation. Ashika straps a large basket to her head and starts to pick leaves. She must work until four in the afternoon and pick eighteen kilograms for a day's pay. Show pupils the leaf and ask them to feel how light it is. Show the weight and ask them to feel how heavy it is. Imagine how many leaves Ashika has to pick for them to weigh eighteen kilograms. For this Ashika earns 80 pence a day! Even then, her day is not over. Ashika has to go home to cook and clean for her family.

You can now buy teas with

the 'Fair Trade' mark. This mark tells you that the pickers have been paid a fair price for their work. One such tea is 'Clipper Tea'. Cafod is a Catholic agency that supports tea pickers in Sri Lanka, helping them to campaign for fair and just living and working conditions and fair wages. People in this country can support the tea pickers by buying tea with a 'Fair Trade' mark. (See page 93.)

Prayer/Reflection
Pour out a cup of tea and ask the pupils to think of all that went into making it. Read the biblical material and the reflection.

As we look at this liquid, we think of people like Ashika who work hard to produce it.
We pray for all those who are working for better conditions on the tea plantations and ask that we may do our part.

Music suggestions
'Now we sing a harvest song' and 'Sad, puzzled eyes.' The Complete Come and Praise, comp.
G. Marshall-Taylor (BBC 1990)

'At Table.' Rejoice 1, comp. A. White, A. Byrne and C. Malone (Harper Collins Religious 1993)

Information taken from 'Fairground' Issue 8 produced by Cafod, 2 Romero Close Stockwell SW9 9TY.

Biblical material

Mark 6.31; Matthew 26.36

Come with me to a quiet place and get some rest.

Jesus went to pray in a garden called Gethsemane, as he often did.

You will need

A newspaper and a radio

Introduction

Before the assembly, arrange for two pupils/staff to enter having an argument and others to enter playing a radio, when you give them the cue. Explain to the pupils that you are in need of a rest. Ask them to be quiet while you read the newspaper. Enter staff/ pupils with a loud radio, disturbing your peace. Ask them to be quiet, explain you need a rest. As soon as they are quiet the other pupils can enter having an argument. Again ask for some peace and quiet. Ask pupils for suggestions concerning where you could go for peace and rest.

Core material

We all need times of rest and quiet. Jesus often went out into the countryside - by himself or with his disciples- to pray and think. He used to go to an olive grove (garden of olive trees) called Gethsemane. He went there to pray just before he died.

Sometimes it is difficult to find somewhere quiet. There is a lot of noise from traffic, radios and other people. Christians like to have quiet places to pray. Sometimes Christians pray in church when it is empty. The empty, quiet, stillness helps them to concentrate. Sometimes Christians create a quiet place at home where they can be alone with God. Some Christians like to follow Jesus' example and pray outdoors where nature can help them think about God. An organisation called 'The Quiet Garden Trust' uses gardens for this purpose. Sometimes a person will open their own home and garden on a regular basis and let other people use it for prayer and reflection. Other gardens are especially created and there are now over fifty 'Quiet Gardens' in different parts of the world.

Prayer/Reflection

Ask pupils to sit with eyes closed in silence. Ask them to think about where they would go if they wanted some peace and quiet and/or read the prayer if appropriate.

God who is present in the busy city and noisy street,
Hear us in the silence.
God who is present in the shout of the playground,
Hear us in the silence.
God who is present in the sounds of our cities,
Hear us in the silence.

Music suggestions

Play the 'Sound of Silence' by Simon and Garfunkel for the pupils to enter and leave.

'When God made the garden of Creation.' The Complete Come and Praise comp. G. Marshall-Taylor (BBC 1990)

'Time to be still.' Come and Praise, Beginning, comp. G. Marshall-Taylor and D. Coombes (BBC 1996)

Note: 'Quiet Learning' is a special project of the Quiet Garden Trust which is being developed for teachers and pupils. The Quiet Garden Trust, Stoke Park Farm, Park Road, Stoke Poges, Bucks. SL2 4PG.

Biblical material
Revelation 14.6

I looked up and saw an angel flying in the heavens with a message from God to proclaim to all the people of the earth, of every tongue, tribe and nation.

You will need
Food, or pictures of food, from various countries

A map or globe (optional)

Introduction
Encourage pupils to bring and show the different foods and ask the rest of the school/class which country produced them. If you have a map show them where that country is. Ask pupils how the goods get from one country to another. Explain that the crops are harvested in one country then often moved by ship to another. This allows us to enjoy a wide range of foods that we cannot grow ourselves. If we had to rely only on what we could produce, there would be no oranges, bananas or chocolate. Ask what some of the items brought in by pupils might cost. There is a human 'cost' to the harvest. The seamen transport the harvest of many countries around the world and have to travel far from home where they have no friends and family.

Core material
If seamen are ill, sad or lonely a Christian organisation called The Missions to Seamen helps. The Missions to Seamen has over 100 Centres in ports across the world and over 300 chaplains. The staff of the Centres provide leisure facilities, a shop, food, telephones for the sailors to phone home, but most of all a friendly welcome, a listening ear and practical help. The Centre chaplains visit ships, take church services, provide transport and visit seamen in hospital if they are taken ill. In the course of one year the Mission staff will visit over 2000 sick seamen. If there are problems the Mission staff try to sort them out. Here is one case the Mission dealt with.

'A Filipino sailor was taken seriously ill in Australia. He had only been married for three months and his wife was far away in Hong Kong. Within a few hours, the Hong Kong Centre had contacted the sailor's wife and paid for a flight to Australia so that she was with her husband.' Australian chaplain.

The flying angel is the symbol of The Missions to Seamen. They chose this symbol from a verse in the Bible. Read the Biblical material. The Missions to Seamen help anyone, of any faith or country. They feel they are called to proclaim (spread) God's message of love and justice to the seamen who transport our food. They believe the best way to do that is to show that love and justice in action.

Prayer/Reflection
Pupils can list the contents of a burger and create a prayer ending each line with we thank you God.

For wheat from Britain
For meat and lettuce from Europe
For cheese from Ireland
For pickles from Germany
For onions from America
We thank you Heavenly Father for all those involved in the world's harvests: those who grow the food and those who transport it.

Music suggestions
'We thank you Lord.' Come and Praise 2, comp. G. Marshall-Taylor (BBC 1988)

'Praise God for the harvest.' Praise God Together, comp. M. Old (Scripture Union 1984)

NOTE: this assembly can be split into two assemblies for younger children or those with special needs. One about where food comes from and one on The Missions to Seamen.

With thanks to The Missions to Seamen, St Michael Paternoster Royal, College Hill, London, EC4R 2RL
With thanks also to Macdonalds for supplying the above information.

You will need

A kitchen timer
A paper 'dipstick' (photocopy the one provided)

Introduction

People sometimes say, ' I went flying to the rescue!' (Ask pupils what this means.) They don't mean that they really flew: they mean that they moved very quickly to help someone in trouble! Sometimes, help is needed very quickly: if it doesn't arrive in time, it will be no help at all to the people waiting for it. Some people really do 'fly to the rescue'! They are the pilots who fly planes for MAF, the Mission Aviation Fellowship. They are a group of Christians who fly planes to help others. One of their planes takes off every four minutes. (Ask a pupil to set the timer for four minutes.) So if one took off now, another would be taking off when this timer goes off. Listen for this, but don't say anything when it goes off. But sometimes they do not 'fly to the rescue' straightaway: instead, they do a sum!

Core material

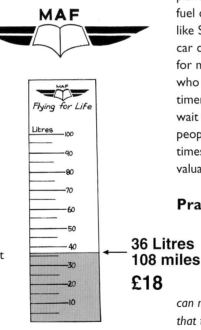

One day in Tanzania, a six year old boy called Stephano became very ill. He could hardly breathe, and his mother realised that she had to find help for him. She strapped him to her back, and set off with a few friends on the long walk through the wild countryside to the nearest hospital - eleven miles away! It was night time: there were no street lights - and the small group could hear lions nearby! At last, they arrived at the hospital - and found out that no one there could help them! Stephano was dying: but the hospital did not have the equipment to help him. But there was one hope: perhaps the plane belonging to MAF could get there in time. Stephano's mother waited: her son was getting worse. Surely the plane would arrive soon?

But the pilot had not set off straightaway! Instead, he had sat down - and did some mathematics! And Stephano's mother was still waiting! But, you see, the pilot had to make sure that he had just the right amount of fuel. If he had too little, the plane would not arrive back safely once he had picked up Stephano and his mother and a doctor. If he had too much fuel, then the weight of that with the weight of the people would be too much - and the little plane would not be able to fly at all! As soon as he had finished the sum, he used a dipstick (like this one) - just like the ones we use in this country to measure how much oil we have in our cars - to make sure that he had just the right amount of fuel in the tank. Then he set off. He collected Stephano and his mother and a doctor, and took them to a big city hospital where they had the right equipment. And there, the doctors found a bead from a necklace stuck in the little boy's lung. Stephano was safe!

Hold up the paper dipstick, and show how a small amount of fuel - just 36 litres - is enough for a MAF plane to fly 108 miles. And this only costs £18! This fuel could be enough to save the life of another child like Stephano. It could fly a doctor to a village that a car could not reach, where many people were waiting for medicine. It could take an eye doctor to people who needed an operation to restore their sight. (If the timer has not yet gone off, draw attention to it, and wait for it.) MAF has 183 planes waiting to help people. They work in 31 countries, and take off 360 times a day. Fuel is fairly cheap for us: but it can be so valuable that it saves the lives of others.

Prayer/Reflection

Pupils can listen quietly while the prayer is read.

Father, help us to remember that sometimes something small - a few coins, a smile, a letter - can make a lot of difference to other people. Thank you that the pilots of MAF work hard to bring help to others.

Music suggestions

'Caring, sharing' and 'God has given us eyes to see.' Big Blue Planet, ed. J. Jarvis (Stainer and Bell Ltd. and Methodist Church Division of Education and Youth 1995)

With thanks to The Mission Aviation Fellowship, Ingles Manor, Castle Hill Avenue, Folkestone, Kent CT20 2TN.

Biblical material

The story of Ruth: Ruth 1-2

The story of David and Goliath: I Samuel 17

The story of Christmas: Matthew 1.18 - 2.12; Luke 1.26-38; 2.1-20

You will need

A children's Bible

Introduction

Talk about 999 calls and what the signal SOS is used for. It can be remembered by the phrase 'save our souls.' Discuss what the different rescue services rescue people from. These stories are all about people who saved or rescued others. Ruth saved Naomi by working hard in the fields to support her. She rescued Naomi from hunger and loneliness. David saved Israel from the Philistines. Jesus is called the Saviour by Christians, the person who saves people from wrong.

Core material

The name Bethlehem means 'House of Bread'. Bethlehem is a small place with a big history. We are going to look at three stories associated with it. These stories can be used as a preliminary to Christmas, or the first story can be used for Harvest.

1) Bethlehem is associated with Ruth and Naomi. Naomi and her family left Bethlehem because there was a famine. The whole family moved to Moab and there Naomi's sons married two Moabite girls called Ruth and Orpah. Later, after her husband and her sons had died, Naomi returned to Bethlehem with her daughter-in-law, Ruth. Naomi had tried hard to persuade Ruth to stay in Moab where she would be well looked after, but Ruth insisted in coming with her to Bethlehem. Ruth worked hard in the fields, picking up grain which the workers dropped, in order to feed Naomi and herself. She eventually married a local farmer called Boaz. Their great grandson was King David.

2) David, Ruth's great grandson, was the youngest of eight brothers. One day he left the town to take bread and cheese to his brothers who were away fighting the Philistines. It was then he met the huge Philistine, Goliath. David heard Goliath boasting and decided he would fight him. At first people laughed at David: he was only a young shepherd boy with no military training. Finally, the king decided to let him go into battle and gave him his own armour. David found he could not move wearing heavy armour, so he took it off and went to meet Goliath armed only with his shepherd's sling and his trust in God. Goliath jeered at the sight of David, but a stone from David's sling, hurled at great speed, hit him on the forehead and Goliath fell, dead.

3) The most well known story associated with Bethlehem is the birth of Jesus. Joseph was a descendant of David (and Ruth) and had to return to Bethlehem to be taxed. Mary, expecting Jesus, gave birth in Bethlehem, fulfilling the prophecy that a great king would be born there. Micah 5.2:

'You, Bethlehem, in the land of Judah, although you are a little town, out of you shall come a great ruler.'

Prayer/Reflection

Ask pupils to close their eyes and think of the town of Bethlehem and what happened there.

Bethlehem: for thousands of years it saw ordinary people growing up. It also knew great rescuers: Ruth's quiet rescue of Naomi, David's brave rescue of Israel and the birth of Jesus who rescued people from wrong.

Music suggestions

'Come, come, come to the manger.' A Year of Celebration, ed. J. Porter and J. McCrimmon (McCrimmons 1995)

'I am the Bread of Life.' (ibid.)

'Christ was born in Bethlehem.' Big, Blue Planet, ed. J. Jarvis (Stainer and Bell Ltd and Methodist Church Division of Education and Youth 1995)

Assembly 70. Bethany: The Place of Rest

Biblical material
John 12.1-8

Before the Passover, Jesus went to Bethany, which was the home of his friends Mary, Martha and their brother Lazarus. Martha had prepared a meal for them and Lazarus was with Jesus. Mary took a very expensive bottle of perfume and poured it over Jesus' feet. She wiped his feet with her long hair and the house was filled with the smell of the perfume. Judas, one of Jesus' disciples, grumbled, 'What a waste, that perfume could have been sold and given to the poor.' Judas did not really care about the poor. He looked after the money and often stole some for himself. It was Judas who betrayed Jesus to his enemies. 'Leave her alone,' said Jesus. 'She has done this because she knows I am about to die. You will always have the poor to care for, but I will only be with you for a little while.'

You will need
A bottle of perfume (do not open)
A novel or bottle of bubble bath

Introduction
Talk about needing to rest. Ask children about different ways of relaxing. Some people relax in the bath, some people relax watching TV. Others relax with a good book. Ask pupils to share different ways they have of relaxing. Put your feet up on a chair and get out a novel, or show other ways you relax.

Core material
We all need to relax. Jesus was no different to anyone else in that respect. He needed somewhere to unwind. It is difficult to relax with strangers: we relax best with people we know, in places where we feel we can do what we like. Jesus had close friends whom he knew well enough to be able to relax in their company. They were a family made up of two sisters and a brother, and they lived in Bethany near Jerusalem. Their names were Martha, Mary and Lazarus. During the last week of Jesus' life, just before the Easter events, Jesus used to spend the days in Jerusalem and then come 'home' to Bethany at night. The story from the Bible tells of an unusual incident that happened while he was relaxing with his friends.

Read the story and show the perfume. Talk about how much it cost. The perfume Mary used would have been worth a year's wages to a poor person. Judas was right - it could have been sold and the money used to help others, yet Jesus defends Mary's 'waste'. It was not that Jesus was uncaring about the poor: he had spent his whole life serving them. He recognised that his friend, Mary, had understood what he was about to do, and she needed to show her love and her sadness at his coming death. Jesus recognised the real friendship of Mary and the false friendship of Judas.

Prayer/Reflection
Stand the jar of perfume on the table. Ask pupils to look at the perfume and think about the love and friendship it stood for in the story. Ask them to close their eyes and think of their own friends and any objects they might have that remind them of their friendship.

Music suggestions
'Said Judas to Mary.' or 'I will bring you the best gift I can offer.' The Complete Come and Praise, comp. G. Marshall-Taylor (BBC 1990)

'Thank you God for all our friends.' Come and Praise Beginning, comp. G. Marshall-Taylor and D. Coombes (BBC 1996)

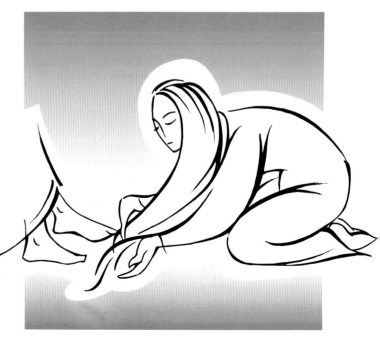

Biblical material

The Lost Sheep (page 88) and Luke 15.1-7

Introduction

This can be a class led assembly. By using a narrator and chorus, everyone can be involved. A teacher or pupil can take the part of the narrator. The sketch can be followed by a Bible reading/s if desired. Gestures should be large and expressive. Individual 'actors' can step out of the chorus and mime while the chorus speaks.

Core material

The Parable of the Good Newsagent
by Jon Webster

Narrator There was once an old newsagent who ran a corner shop.

Chorus Open all hours! (With a northern accent)

Narrator One day Albert - that was his name - had a new paper-boy.

Chorus Wayne's the name. (All wave)

Narrator Wayne was really keen to get started.

Chorus I'm saving for a mountain bike. (Mime riding)

Narrator Albert tried to give him directions for his paper-round.

Chorus (All children, individually, mutter directions like 'go right, then left, then second right, then...' At the same time they wave their arms around.)

Narrator But Wayne, the new paperboy, was too excited to listen.

Chorus Seeya! Back soon! (Wave)

Narrator The old newsagent tried to warn him.

Chorus Hang about! (Beckon with arm)

Narrator But it was too late.

Chorus (Fold arms, shake head)

Narrator Wayne was gone... Then the fog came down. Old Mrs Jones came in for a Radio Times.

Chorus I'm stoppin' in tonight. (Croaky voice)

Narrator And the fog got thicker. But where was Wayne? P.C. Plod came in for throat sweets.

Chorus 'Ello, 'ello, 'ello! (Policeman's knee-bending, hands behind back routine) It's a regular pea-souper.

Narrator And the fog got thicker. But where was Wayne? Mavis came in for some crisps.

Chorus They've stopped the buses. The drivers can't see! (Much shrugging of shoulders)

Narrator And the fog got thicker still. But where was Wayne? At last the old newsagent put on his cap...

Chorus (Mime)

Narrator ...and his scarf.

Chorus (Mime)

Narrator His wife didn't want him to go.

Chorus Think of your chest.

Narrator It was true. The doctor had said:

Chorus It could kill you. (Wag finger)

Narrator But he wouldn't listen. All he knew was that Wayne was

Chorus lost. (Plaintive cry)

Narrator He went out in the foggy streets, calling:

Chorus Wayne? Wayne? (Hands cupped to mouth)

Narrator No reply. He tried again...

Chorus Wayne! Wayne!

Narrator Still no reply.

Chorus Wayne! Wayne! (Starts coughing)

Narrator Then he heard a small voice, seemingly miles away.

Chorus Help! Mr Higginbotham. I'm lost.

Narrator He struggled through the fog, his lungs aching.

Chorus Come on, Wayne! I think we deserve a nice cuppa tea.

Narrator And so they delivered the papers together and got safely home.

Chorus (Mimes pushing papers in letter boxes) We'll make a paper-boy of you yet!

Prayer/Reflection

Ask some pupils to play a quiet tune on the recorder while pupils close their eyes and think about being lost. Pupils might like to finish the time of reflection with their own prayers written for the occasion.

Music suggestions

'Lost and Found.' The Complete Come and Praise, comp. G. Marshall-Taylor (BBC 1990)

'The Lord, the Lord.' Come and Praise Beginning, comp. G. Marshall-Taylor and D. Coombes (BBC 1996)

Biblical material
Luke 15. 8-10

There was once a woman who had ten coins. She was not rich and the coins meant a lot to her. One day, to her horror, she discovered one was missing. She searched through the house. She lifted boxes and swept the floor. She looked in corners and under beds. All day she searched until she found it. When she did find it, she was so overjoyed that she invited her neighbours in to celebrate. In the same way, God is overjoyed when one person becomes his friend.

You will need
Party hats, streamers or other party items

Introduction
Encourage pupils to talk about parties they have attended. Ask some pupils to try on the hats and demonstrate the other party items. Explain that today's story is about a party, but what sort of party is it? A birthday party? A wedding party? Ask the pupils to guess.

Core material
Start at the end of the story. 'Today's story is about a woman who threw a party. It was not her birthday. It was not a wedding or to celebrate the birth of a baby. It was not a going away party or a homecoming. It was not a house-warming for a new home. It was a "found" party.'

The woman had lost something that was very important to her. She was so relieved that she threw a party to celebrate finding it. Read the biblical material.

Many of us have lost money at some time. You may have lost your dinner money or some pocket money. Most of us do not throw a party when we find it. To understand this story Jesus told, we need to know a little about life at the time.

Many people were quite poor. When people grew old, there was no money (pension) from the government. If people were ill, there were no hospitals, and doctors cost money. Without money, people could starve.

Most people tried to save a little for 'hard' times. This woman had ten coins saved, which was not very much. It was about ten days' wages. This meant the family could survive for ten days if they were ill or could not work for some other reason. The coins were small. It would have been hard searching in the house: there would only have been a little light from the doorway and the windows were small. The woman would have used a small dish lamp to look for the coin, but the lamps gave off a very weak light. Despite the difficulties, the woman kept looking until she found it. She did not give up: the coin mattered to her - it was important. When she did find the coin, she invited the neighbours to join her celebration. She threw a party.

This story was told by Jesus to remind people that God thinks every person is important, just as the coin was important to the woman, and that he celebrates when a person becomes his friend.

Prayer/Reflection
Blow some of the party whistles and throw some streamers. Ask pupils to think about things which they celebrate. This story reminds Christians that God celebrates when people become his friends.

Music suggestions
'Lost and Found.' The Complete Come and Praise, comp. G. Marshall-Taylor (BBC 1990)
'Lost and Found.' Rejoice 1, comp. A. White, A. Byrne and C. Malone (Harper Collins Religious 1993)

Story: The Prodigal Son

There was once a farmer who had two sons. The elder son worked hard on the farm, but his brother was bored. One day, he went to his father. 'When you die', he said, 'I will receive my share of your money. Give it to me now, while I can enjoy it. I can't bear to live here like this any longer.' His father was sad when he heard this. He did not want his son to leave home, but he realised that the boy would not be happy if he stayed. So he gave him the money, and watched as he left home.

The boy travelled a long way until he came to a great city. There he found somewhere to live, and bought expensive food and clothes. He organised parties each evening, and many people came to enjoy the free food and drink! But soon his money ran out. His 'friends' did not want to know him, and he was left alone, without a place to live or food to eat. In desperation, he took a job on a farm, looking after pigs. But he was always hungry and very lonely.

One day he could stand it no longer. 'I'm going home,' he decided. 'My father's servants live better than this! I don't deserve to live as dad's son any more: but I'll say sorry for wasting his money, and beg him to let me work for him.'

So off he set. As he trudged along the dusty track leading to the farm, he saw someone running towards him. He shaded his eyes, trying to see who it was. Had his father sent someone to drive him away? But - it looked like his father himself! And it was him! He threw his arms round his son. 'At last!' he cried. 'Every day I have watched for you, longing to see you again. And you're here, safe and sound!' His father took him home. He wouldn't even listen when he tried to say sorry. He told his servants to help his son bathe and dress. 'Get a great feast ready to celebrate his return,' he said. Then he put a ring on his son's finger. 'Welcome home, son,' he said.

When the elder son returned from his hard day's work, he was amazed to hear the party in the house. 'What's happening?' he asked. When he was told, he was furious. He stormed off into the night. His father came out to see what was wrong. 'You never did this - or anything - for me!' his son shouted. 'Yet I have worked faithfully for you all these years - not like that brother of mine!'

'But son,' his father said patiently, 'you are always here with me, and all that I have will be yours one day. But I thought your brother was dead - and here he is! He was lost - but now he's found! That is why we are celebrating.'

Story for use with page 85

Story: The Lost Sheep

It was a hard life, out on the hills around the village. The nights were cold, and the wolves howled round the little camp as the shepherd lay, wrapped in his cloak, across the entrance of the sheep-fold. He had never lost a sheep to a wolf or to a mountain-lion, but it had been a close thing at times. Only his bravery and skill with the sling had kept his animals safe. Several of his friends had lost sheep to the wild animals. Even without that danger, life wasn't easy. Every morning, he gathered his flock together, and set off at its head to find fresh grass and gently flowing streams for them. He led them along steep drops and through rocky valleys, talking to them, helping them over rough ground and through thorns with his staff. And always he was watching out for danger.

One night, as he counted them into the fold, he realised that one sheep was missing. Which one was it? He looked closely at the sheep as they began to settle for the night. Yes, now he knew which one it was - the young ewe which always seemed to think she knew the best way to go, not him! Quickly he gathered up loose stones, and blocked the entrance to the fold as well as he could. The rest would be safe in there. Then he picked up his staff and set off.

At first, it wasn't too difficult: he knew the paths well. But soon they became unfamiliar. He stumbled over rocks, and caught his cloak and hands on thorns. He heard rustlings, and imagined wild animals, desperate for food, creeping up on him. Still he struggled on, the thought of giving up never crossing his mind. And, at last, he heard an answering bleat - far off but unmistakable. He followed the sound, and found the ewe caught by her fleece in a tangle of thorn bushes. She was pleased to see him! He carefully released her, and hoisted her onto his shoulders and set off, back to the fold. 'I'll have to celebrate,' he told her. 'I thought I'd lost you, and here you are, safe and sound!' And he walked on happily, deciding who he was going to ask to his party.

Story for use with page 50

Story: Manna in the Desert

The people of Israel were not happy! They grumbled to Moses that they were starving! Moses shook his head sadly. These people forgot what it was like being slaves. They forgot the beatings and only remembered the food! He told God all about it, and God told him what he would do. 'God is going to send you bread, ' Moses told them. 'It will fall down like rain every morning! And he will send meat for you too, every evening! Then you will know that God is still looking after you.' That evening, small birds called quail flew in and settled all around the camp. The Israelites easily caught enough for everyone.

Next morning, when they got up, they found the ground was covered with small flakes of something. 'What is it?' they asked each other. Someone was brave enough to taste it. He said, 'It's good! It tastes like wafers made with honey!' Then they all tried it, and it was good! This was the bread that God sent for them to eat in the desert. God sent it every day until they were able to find other food in the new land he had promised to give them.

Story for use with page 56

Story: Feeding the 5,000

People enjoyed listening to Jesus. They enjoyed it so much that they forgot what time it was! Now it was getting late, and the disciples were worried. 'Look at all these people!' they said. 'They're tired and hungry. How can we find them all something to eat before they walk home?'

Jesus asked the disciples how much food they had. They had only got five small loaves and two fishes and there were 5,000 men as well as all the women and children! Jesus took the food in his hands. He looked up, and prayed, thanking God for the food he had given them. Then he began to break the bread and fish into small pieces. The disciples took the pieces from him, and gave them to the crowd. They did this over and over until everyone had eaten enough. Then the disciples picked up all the food that had been dropped - and this filled twelve baskets! The disciples were amazed!

89

Song for use with page 65

Alleluia

Traditional
South African

Arranged by Gobingca George Mxadana. This version comes from World Praise edited by D. Peacock and G. Weaver (Marshall Pickering 1993).

Story for use with page 66

Story: Good Friday

Jesus' enemies seemed to have won. They had plotted to get him killed, and here he was, dying on the cross. But even as he died, Jesus was thinking about other people. He asked God to forgive the men who were killing him. He asked his friend John to look after Mary, his mother, for him. And he told a thief who was dying with him that he was now God's friend. For Jesus knew that he, Jesus, was dying for a good reason. He wanted to help all these people - his friends, his enemies, the ones who had just come to watch. He wanted to help them become friends with God, and rescue them from wrong.

When he realised that he was about to die, he shouted out, 'I have done it!' And then he died. A Roman officer was watching. When he heard this cry he understood that this was not an ordinary man. 'Surely this was the Son of God!' he said.

Picture for use with page 39

CHRISTIAN

Picture for use with page 40

DANGER

The Swamp of Sadness

Picture for use with page 59

Information for use with pages 27 and 61

El Salvador

El Salvador is a land of mountains and valleys. The land is very
fertile in the valleys. Coffee, sugar, cotton, oranges, bananas, rice,
beans and maize can be grown. El Salvador is a small crowded
country. It is about the size of Wales but has five million people.
Almost one out of every three people does not have a job. Two
out of every three adults cannot read. Most people are very
poor, but a few people are very rich. El Salvador has suffered
from civil war - two groups within the country fought each other
for many years. A peace treaty was eventually signed in 1992.
During the civil war, more than 70,000 people were killed.

Useful Addresses:

Cafod, 2 Romero Close, Stockwell Road, London SW9 9TY.
Christian Aid, PO Box 100, London SE1 7RT.
Trocaire, 169 Booters Town, Black Rock, Dublin.
SCIAF, 5 Oswald Street, Glasgow, G14 QR.

Trademark for use with page 79. **NOT TO BE PHOTOCOPIED.** (Reproduced with permission)

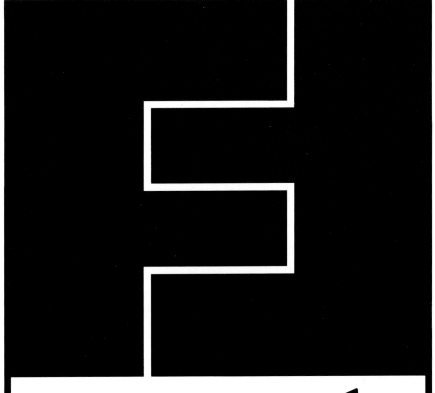

Fairtrade
Guarantees a **better deal** for Third World Producers

A termly magazine for Primary Schools

The 72 assemblies in this book have been taken from the first six issues of the *Cracking RE* magazine published from the Autumn Term 1996 to the Summer Term 1998.

Cracking RE has been designed with the needs of the busy classroom teacher in mind. Each issue is packed full of practical ideas for teaching Christianity and for leading assemblies. *Cracking RE* builds into a comprehensive resource which can be used time and time again. It supports the Christianity requirements of RE syllabuses throughout the UK. *Cracking RE* is published once a term.

To order *Cracking RE* for the current or forthcoming academic year, at a cost of £28 for 3 issues, please complete the form below.

Name and address to which *Cracking RE* should be sent (if paying by credit card this must be the address at which the card is registered):

Order details (please tick ONE box):
- ☐ Please send me an inspection copy

- ☐ I wish to subscribe to *Cracking RE* for the school year beginning in Autumn 19___
  Payment details (please tick ONE box):
  - ☐ I enclose a cheque (made payable to *The Stapleford Centre*)
  - ☐ Please send me an invoice
  - ☐ Please debit my Visa/Mastercard/Delta/Switch card, number _____
    Expiry date _____   Issue number _____

Signed _____   Date _____

Photocopy this form and send it to: The Stapleford Centre, Stapleford House, Wesley Place, Stapleford, Nottingham NG9 8DP. Tel. (0115) 939 6270. Fax. (0115) 939 2076. Email: admin@stapleford-centre.org

Services for Primary Schools offered by The Stapleford Centre

Cracking Assemblies is published by the Stapleford Centre, other books for primary schools produced by the Centre are:

Jesus through Art

24 A3 colour prints with pupil activities covering the life and teaching of Jesus. Includes comprehensive notes for the teacher and photocopiable stories and worksheets for pupils (7-11 years).

Haffertee Handbook

The adventures of a toy hamster are used to teach Christianity to 5-7 year olds - comprehensive teachers' manual. To be used in conjunction with the Haffertee Story Books: *Haffertee Hamster, Haffertee's First Christmas* and *Haffertee's First Easter*.

Wisdom for Worship

Contains 70 reflective assemblies based on the Book of Proverbs.

Toolkit 3 volume set

Creative ideas for using the Bible in the classroom for the non-specialist.

Volume 1	*Writing and Poetry*
Volume 2	*Story and Drama*
Volume 3	*Art and Music*

Postbag from Palestine

17 New Testament stories retold using faxes, postcards, letters and telephone messages. Includes background notes, conversation guides, activities and assemblies. Photocopiable.

Mailbag from the Middle East

20 Old Testament stories retold using using faxes, postcards, letters and telephone messages. Includes background notes, conversation guides, activities and assemblies. Photocopiable.

Ten Minute Miracle Plays

12 plays based on the medieval Miracle Play cycles provide a simple reading or a fully staged performance, to bring the Bible to life.

Faith in History

54 topics drawing together RE and history in one comprehensive teacher hand book.

Plus photocopiable Worksheets:

Invaders and Settlers
Tudors and Stuarts
Victorian Britain
Britain after 1930
Full Set (52 Worksheets)

REsource Banks

Bible stories accompanied by photocopiable activity sheets and background notes. Eight topics per volume.

Volume 1: Includes friends, families, mending friendships, sharing, forgiveness, trust

Volume 2: Includes living wisely, laws for living, opposites, promises, change, peace

Volume 3: Includes messages from God, Jesus, Prayer, The Holy Spirit

Christianity Topic Books

Photocopiable cross curricular ideas for teaching Christianity as a living faith.

Volume 1 - Autumn Term
Volume 2 - Spring Term
Volume 3 - Summer Term

Assemblies for Primary Schools

Simple, imaginative and practical ideas for assemblies.

Autumn Term
Spring Term
Summer Term

The Final Journey : An Easter play

Photocopiable scripts - 7 short scenes with 25 different speaking parts.

The Centre also offers a range of distance learning courses in Religious Education, validated by the University of Nottingham. Ideal for subject leaders.

Order form

☐ Copy/copies Jesus through Art @ £24.95	£
☐ Copy/copies Cracking Assemblies £ @ £12.95	£
☐ Copy/copies Haffertee Handbook @ £30	£
☐ Copy/copies of Haffertee Hamster @ £2.99	£
☐ Copy/copies of Haffertee's First Christmas @ £2.99	£
☐ Copy/copies of Haffertee's First Easter @ £2.99	£
☐ Copy/copies Wisdom for Worship @ £11.95	£
☐ Copy/copies Toolkit 3 volume set @ £35.99 (while stocks last)	£
☐ Copy/copies Toolkit: Writing and Poetry @ £13.99	£
☐ Copy/copies Toolkit: Story and Drama @ £13.95	£
☐ Copy/copies Toolkit: Art and Music @ £13.99	£
☐ Copy/copies Postbag from Palestine @ £15.00	£
☐ Copy/copies Mailbag from the Middle East @ £17.50	£
☐ Copy/copies Ten Minute Miracle Plays @ £15.99	£
☐ Copy/copies Faith in History @ £25.00	£
☐ Copy/copies Faith in History Worksheets complete set @ £24.96	£
☐ Copy/copies Invaders and Settlers 22 Worksheets @ £9.99	£

☐ Copy/copies Tudors and Stuarts 11 Worksheets @ £4.99	£
☐ Copy/copies Victorian Britain 10 Worksheets @ £4.99	£
☐ Copy/copies Britain After 1930 10 Worksheets @ £4.99	£
☐ Copy/copies REsource Bank 1 @ £14.95	£
☐ Copy/copies REsource Bank 2 @ £14.95	£
☐ Copy/copies REsource Bank 3 @ £14.95	
☐ Copy/copies Christianity Topic Book 1 @ £13.95	£
☐ Copy/copies Christianity Topic Book 2 @ £13.95	£
☐ Copy/copies Christianity Topic Book 3 @ £13.95	£
☐ Copy/copies Assemblies for Primary Schools Autumn term @ £8.95	£
☐ Copy/copies Assemblies for Primary Schools Spring term @ £8.95	£
☐ Copy/copies Assemblies for Primary Schools Summer term @ £8.95	£
☐ Copy/copies The Final Journey @ £10.50	£
Total £	

The Centre also offers a range of distance learning courses in Religious Education validated by the University Of Nottingham.

Tick here for more details ☐

I enclose an official order form / cheque / credit card details (please delete as appropriate).
Cheques should be made payable to **The Stapleford Centre**
Post Orders to: The Stapleford Centre, Stapleford House, Wesley Place, Stapleford, Nottingham, NG9 8DP
Telephone orders: 0115 939 6270; Fax orders to: 0115 939 2076. e-mail orders to: admin@stapleford-centre.org
VAT number: 695 1265 12

Please Debit my Access/Visa/Switch/Delta account.

Card no: _____ Expiry date: _____ Issue no. _____

Cardholder Name and Initials _____

Signature _____ Date _____

Name _____ Address _____

_____

_____ Tel _____